Whatever H
to the
Ten Commandments?

Whatever Happened to the Ten Commandments?

Ernest C. Reisinger

THE BANNER OF TRUTH TRUST

THE BANNER OF TRUTH TRUST
3 Murrayfield Road, Edinburgh EH12 6EL
P. O. Box 621, Carlisle, Pennsylvania 17013, USA

*

© E.C. Reisinger 1999
First published 1999
ISBN 0 85151 763 3

*

*

Typeset in 12/13 pt Sabon MT at
The Banner of Truth Trust,
Edinburgh
Printed in Great Britain by
Bell & Bain Ltd.,
Glasgow

Author's Foreword

Today's lack of concern about the Ten Commandments, not to mention ignorance of what they are, is traceable to the secularization of society which has sought to destroy any absolute standard for behaviour. Educational systems in the western world have attempted, over the last fifty years, to establish an amoral society. The fruit of this is now seen in the home, the school, the college, the work-place, and ever so clearly in the political arena. Doing whatever pleases oneself is the norm (see *Judg.* 17:5–6). This state of affairs is well described by the evangelical prophet: 'Woe to those who call evil good, and good evil; who put darkness for light, and light for darkness; who put bitter for sweet, and sweet for bitter' (*Isa.* 5:20).

The professing church is largely to blame for this decline. Modern theology has cut itself adrift from the pattern of righteousness found in the Decalogue. But equally serious is what some evangelical churches have done to the law of God. They have emphasized the love of God at the expense of his holiness and have not shown unbelievers his hatred of sin nor believers his demand for righteousness. The result is that the sins of society are also found in many churches.

The material in these studies is not original. I am indebted to the Rev. Glen Charles Knecht's sermons on the Ten Commandments preached in the First Presbyterian Church, Columbia, South Carolina. But the principal sources which I have used are Francis Turretin's *Institutes of Elenctic Theology,* Thomas Watson's *Commentary on the Ten Commandments*, Robert Shaw's *Exposition of the Westminster Confession of Faith* and, in particular, *The Larger Catechism of the Westminster Assembly*. Sadly, the *Larger Catechism* has taken a secondary place to the *Shorter Catechism,* with the result that the detailed questions and answers about the commandments, the church and preaching which it alone contains are overlooked.

The main purpose of these pages is to focus attention on the Ten Commandments and to present the duties required and the sins forbidden in each of them. But before doing that, and by way of introduction, I will emphasize their collective importance, point out how they relate to justification and sanctification and give principles for their right understanding and use.

I pray that these studies will help to establish the absolute standard of righteousness required by our great Creator and Redeemer.

ERNEST C. REISINGER

Contents

Introduction

The moral law was written on Adam's heart at creation. After he fell, it was defaced but not totally obliterated. According to Romans 2:14–15, some faint impressions of its requirements still remain on the hearts of all human beings, just like stubble in a field of wheat or corn after the crop has been harvested.

At Mount Sinai, God graciously gave an explicit record of that perfect moral law in the form of Ten Commandments. They were written by God himself (*Exod.* 32: 15–16), unlike the civil and ceremonial laws which Moses wrote at his direction. Though given to the children of Israel after their deliverance from Egypt, they enshrine what Adam and Eve were expected to observe.

They therefore go back to creation and are authoritative for all people in every time and place. They are a fixed, objective standard of righteousness, and so everyone should be concerned about his or her duty to Almighty God, the Creator and Judge of all the earth, who requires a perfect and perpetual obedience to his revealed will.

A. W. Pink wrote about the uniqueness of the Ten Commandments:

> Their uniqueness appears first in that this revelation of God at Sinai – which was to serve for all coming ages as the grand expression of his holiness and the summation of man's duty – was attended with such awe-inspiring phenomena that the very manner of their publication plainly showed that God Himself assigned to the Decalogue peculiar importance. The Ten Commandments were uttered by God in an audible voice, with the fearful adjuncts of clouds and darkness, thunders and lightnings and the sound of a trumpet, and they were the only parts of Divine Revelation so spoken – none of the ceremonial or civil precepts were thus distinguished. Those Ten Words, and they alone, were written by the finger of God upon tables of stone, and they alone were deposited in the holy ark for safe keeping. Thus, in the unique honor conferred upon the Decalogue itself we may perceive its paramount importance in the Divine government (*The Ten Commandments,* Swengel, Pennsylvania: Reiner Publications, 1961, p. 5).

This is borne out in the preface to the Ten Commandments, 'And God spoke all these words, saying: "*I am* the LORD your God, who brought you out of the land of Egypt, out of the house of bondage"' (*Exod.* 20:1–2). This indicates that the Decalogue is a law of God's own making and disclosing, which stems from his own nature and dealings with his people. He asserts his own authority and presents himself as the sole object of the worship and service which he requires. This is because he is the 'I AM', self-existent and all-determining, and as *the* LORD he is also the Redeemer. He who made all things brought his people out of Egypt, and so they belong to him by a double tie. Thus, love, grace and mercy are all related to the law and we must never totally separate them. Though the commandments themselves are brief, their scope is vast and the whole of Scripture is a commentary on them. The Bible is therefore like a great statute book of God's kingdom, having in it the whole body of heavenly instruction, the perfect rules for a holy life and the gracious promise of eternal life.

The Law's Relationship to Justification and Sanctification

The law and the gospel are the principal themes of divine revelation. Every passage of sacred Scripture is connected, either explicitly or in some related sense, to the one or the other. Even the historical portions of the Old and New Testaments narrate human actions in the light of conformity or opposition to the moral law, or belief or disbelief of the gospel. The ordinances of the ceremonial law, given to the ancient Israelites, were, for the most part, grafted on the Second and Fourth Commandments of the moral law; and in their typical reference, they were an obscure revelation of the gospel. The precepts of the civic law are all reducible to commandments of the moral law, and especially to those of the second table. All threatenings and promises, whether in the Old or in the New Testament, are threatenings or promises attached either to the law or to the gospel. In addition, every prophecy of Scripture is a declaration of future things, connected either with the one or with the other.

As the law and the gospel are the sum and substance of the whole Bible, it is important to relate and distinguish them properly. The clearer our view of the difference between them and their connection with each other, the better will our understanding be of the mind and will of God, and the more useful we will be in his service. But if someone cannot distinguish rightly between them, that person cannot rightly understand or declare divine truth. If he does not have a right and spiritual understanding of the holy law, he cannot have spiritual and transforming discoveries of the glorious gospel; and, on the other hand, if his views of the gospel be erroneous or wrong, his notions of the law cannot be right.

A proper understanding of the difference between the law and the gospel is therefore an essential mark of a minister who rightly divides the Word of truth. Some ministers fail in this task. Charles Bridges says on this:

> The mark of a minister 'approved unto God, a workman that needeth not to be ashamed', is that he 'rightly divides the word of truth'. This implies a full and direct application of the Gospel to the mass of his unconverted hearers, combined with a body of spiritual instruction to the several classes of Christians. His system will be marked by Scriptural symmetry and comprehensiveness. It will embrace the whole revelation of God, in its doctrinal instructions, experimental privileges, and practical results. This revelation is divided into two parts – the Law and the Gospel – essentially distinct from each other, though so intimately connected that an accurate knowledge of neither can be obtained without the other (*The Christian Ministry,* London: Banner of Truth Trust, 1967, p. 222).

The law and the gospel are bound up with the doctrines of justification and sanctification which, in turn, are inseparably joined in the application of God's salvation. But while they cannot be separated, they must be distinguished. Let us therefore be clear on the definition of each of these two basic doctrines and how the law relates to each.

Justification

The answer to Question 70 of The Westminster *Larger Catechism* defines justification as follows:

> Justification is an act of God's free grace unto sinners, in which he pardoneth all their sins, accepteth and accounteth their persons righteous in his sight; not for anything wrought in them, or done by them, but only for the perfect obedience and full satisfaction of Christ, by God imputed to them, and received by faith alone.

Introduction

One may ask, What do the Ten Commandments have to do with our justification? The answer is that they show us that we need a righteousness to stand before God, which we do not have; and, as a schoolmaster (*Gal.* 3:24), they therefore take us to Christ who is our righteousness. The law reveals two things which are necessary to be known for salvation:

1. *The law reveals the character of God*
God's law comes from his nature. It is what God is like that determines what is right, and his will imposes that standard upon all his creatures as a moral obligation. The law is therefore perfect (*Psa.* 19:7), because it reflects the perfection of God's nature.

Man is therefore not answerable to an abstract law, but to God himself. Behind the law is the lawgiver, and to find fault with the former is to malign the latter. The law is not the arbitrary edicts of a capricious despot, but the wise, holy, loving precepts of one who is jealous for his glory and for the good of his people.

2. *The law reveals the condition of man*
Human beings are born disobedient. But to walk up to someone and say, 'All have sinned', does not bring conviction unless that person knows what sin is. As sin is lawlessness (*1 John* 3:4), so knowledge of sin comes by means of the law (*Rom.* 3:20). The knowledge of sin as a personal violation of God's law brings conviction.

In days gone by, children learned the commandments before they learned John 3:16 because only then did John 3:16 have real meaning for them. Likewise, John Eliot's first translation work among the Indians was not of John 3:16 but of the Ten Commandments, and he preached his first sermon on them. Did John Eliot think the Indians would be saved by the Ten Commandments? Of course not, but the commandments would show them why they needed to be saved – they were law-breakers, and they needed a law-keeper to be their substitute.

Similarly, John Paton, the great Presbyterian missionary to the New Hebrides, first taught the commandments. Why? Because people will never be properly interested in a relationship with the Redeemer until they see the terrible breach in their relationship to the Creator. The commandments are the moral mandate of the Creator to creatures. 'The sharp needle of the law makes way for the scarlet thread of the gospel.' The law is indispensable in biblical, God-centred evangelism.

Sanctification
Chapter 13 of the Westminster Confession defines sanctification as follows:

I. They who are effectually called and regenerated, having a new heart and a new spirit created in them, are further sanctified really and personally, through the virtue of Christ's death and resurrection, by his Word and Spirit dwelling in them; the dominion of the whole body of sin is destroyed and the several lusts thereof are more and more weakened and mortified, and they more and more quickened and strengthened in all saving graces, to the practice of true holiness, without which no man shall see the Lord.
II. This sanctification is throughout in the whole man, yet imperfect in this life; there abideth still some remnants of corruption in every part: whence ariseth a continual and irreconcilable war; the flesh lusting against the Spirit and the Spirit against the flesh.
III. In which war, although the remaining corruption for a time may much prevail, yet, through the continual supply of strength from the sanctifying Spirit of Christ, the regenerate part doth overcome: and so the saints grow in grace, perfecting holiness in the fear of God.

But many ask, Can the Ten Commandments have anything to do with sanctification? Was not the law fully abrogated by the coming of Christ into the world? Was not

Christ made under the law in order that he might free his people from it? Does not the New Testament expressly declare that we are not under law but under grace? Is not the attempt to overawe men's consciences by the authority of the Decalogue a legalistic imposition, altogether at variance with that liberty which the Saviour has brought in by his obedience unto death? The answer is that the Lord Jesus Christ himself said, 'Do not think that I came to destroy the Law or the Prophets. I did not come to destroy but to fulfil. For assuredly, I say to you, till heaven and earth pass away, one jot or one tittle will by no means pass from the law till all is fulfilled' and 'Unless your righteousness exceeds the righteousness of the scribes and Pharisees, you will by no means enter the kingdom of heaven' (*Matt.* 5:17–18, 20). It is true that the Christian is not under the moral law as a way of justification, nor as a ministration of condemnation, but he is not free of it as a rule of life, lived in love to the Saviour.

Such a view of the Ten Commandments, therefore, avoids both antinomianism and legalism. The former sees no relationship between the law and the gospel except that of being free; the latter fails to recognise the vital connection between the two. Some preach the law instead of the gospel. Some modify them and preach neither. Some think the law is the gospel, and some think the gospel is the law; those who hold these views are not clear on either.

The relationship between justification and sanctification is summarised in Question 77 of the Westminster *Larger Catechism* as follows:

Q. Wherein do justification and sanctification differ?
A. Although sanctification be inseparably joined with justification, yet they differ in that God in justification imputeth the righteousness of Christ; in sanctification his Spirit infuseth grace, and enableth to the exercise thereof; in the former, sin is pardoned; in the other, it is subdued; the one doth equally free all believers from the revenging wrath

of God, and that perfectly in this life, that they never fall into condemnation; the other is neither equal in all, nor in this life perfect in any, but growing up to perfection.

Robert Murray M'Cheyne made this relationship very clear by saying:

> It is a holy-making gospel. Without holy fruits all evidences are vain. Dear friends, you have awakenings, enlightenings, experiences, and many due signs; but if you lack holiness, you shall never see the Lord. A real desire after complete holiness is the truest mark of being born again. Jesus is a holy Saviour. He first covers the soul with His white raiment, then makes the soul glorious – restores the lost image of God and fills the soul with pure, heavenly holiness. Unregenerate men among you cannot bear this testimony.

There are many good reasons why the doctrines of justification and sanctification should concern every serious Christian:

1. They are the foundation of true conversion.
2. They put repentance back into the evangelistic message.
3. They bear directly on the many self-deceived church members who have walked aisles, troubled baptismal waters, signed decision cards, and had their names entered on church rolls, yet who give no biblical evidence of having been born again by the Holy Spirit. Can a serious-minded person look at present-day church members and not be moved with holy concern and compassion?
4. They deal a death blow to all second-work-of-grace teachings, such as the 'higher life', the 'crucified life' and the 'deeper life', which represent a wrong view of sanctification.
5. They should demolish the notion that one may have Jesus as a Saviour from hell without submitting to him as Lord and that obedience to his precepts is an optional extra.

The duties and sins found in the Ten Commandments teach the need of justification and are also the only fixed, objective standard for sanctified behaviour. The following truth cannot be overemphasized: The working of God's Spirit in our hearts on earth and the cleansing of our sins by Christ's blood in heaven are inseparably joined together in the application of God's salvation. Justification and sanctification always go together in salvation. Any attempt to place the basic act of submission to Christ after conversion cuts the vital nerve of the new covenant and perverts biblical Christianity. To separate these blessings which God has joined together is to bring dishonour on the blood of Christ which was shed to enact the entirety of the new covenant.

Principles for a Right Understanding and Use of the Decalogue

The Ten Commandments must be understood according to the rest of Scripture and not in the light of moral philosophy or social custom. We must not restrict ourselves to a superficial study of the words in which they are expressed but should include material found in other portions of Scripture which is relevant to them. The following are the principles to be followed in studying the Decalogue:

1. The commandments must be understood according to the explanation that the prophets, Christ, and the apostles gave of them.
2. The commandments are spiritual; therefore, they go to the heart and require internal obedience. They require more than outward conformity; they require inward affection. They forbid not only the acts of sin, but the desire and inclination to sin. The Tenth Commandment shows this.
3. There is a positive and a negative side to each of the

commandments. Where a sin is forbidden, a duty is commanded; where a duty is commanded, a sin is implied.
4. Where a sin is forbidden, what leads to that sin is also forbidden.
5. Our understanding of the commandments which deal with relationships between people must be governed by the commandments which deal with our relationship to God. If there seems to be a conflict, our duty to God personally must take precedence.
6. It is essential to remember that the purpose of the commandments is our good as well as God's glory.
7. Whatever is forbidden or commanded we are bound to try to prevent or see performed by others, according to our position in society and our relationship to them.
8. What is forbidden is not to be done at any time, while what is required is always our duty, and especially so at particular times.
9. The beginning and the end, as well as the sum of all the commandments, is love, which is the fulfilment of the law.

These principles will help in a proper understanding of the commandments and will safeguard us from the twin evils of legalism and antinomianism.

Conclusion

Let us ponder the words of four choice spokesmen regarding the law of God:

1. David, a man after God's own heart, the sweet psalmist of Israel, said:

Make me walk in the path of Your commandments,
For I delight in it (*Psa.* 119:35).

Indignation has taken hold of me
Because of the wicked, who forsake Your law (*Psa.* 119:53).

Oh, how I love Your law!
It *is* my meditation all the day (*Psa.* 119:97).

I hate the double-minded,
But I love Your law (*Psa.* 119:113).

It is time for *You* to act, O LORD,
For they have regarded Your law as void (*Psa.* 119:126).

2. Paul, the apostle to the Gentiles:

Do we then make void the law through faith? Certainly not! On the contrary, we establish the law (*Rom.* 3:31).

Therefore the law *is* holy, and the commandment holy and just and good (*Rom.* 7:12).

For I delight in the law of God according to the inward man (*Rom.* 7:22).

Therefore the law was our tutor *to bring us* to Christ, that we might be justified by faith (*Gal.* 3:24).

3. John, the 'apostle of Love':

He who says, 'I know Him,' and does not keep His commandments, is a liar, and the truth is not in him (*1 John* 2:4).

4. Our Lord himself:

Do not think that I came to destroy the Law or the Prophets. I did not come to destroy but to fulfil. For assuredly, I say to you, till heaven and earth pass away, one jot or one tittle will by no means pass from the law till all is fulfilled (*Matt.* 5:17–18).

The First Commandment

You shall have no other gods before Me
(Exod. 20:3).

The following Scriptures will help us in the right under-standing of this First Commandment of the covenant God of Israel, who has visited and redeemed his people:

Thus says the LORD, the King of Israel,
And his Redeemer, the Lord of hosts:
'I *am* the First and I *am* the Last;
Besides Me *there is* no God' (*Isa.* 44:6).

'I appeared to Abraham, to Isaac, and to Jacob, as God Almighty, but *by* My name LORD I was not known to them' (*Exod.* 6:3).

God, who made the world and everything in it, since He is Lord of heaven and earth, does not dwell in temples made with hands . . . for in Him we live and move and have our being, as also some of your own poets have said, 'For we are also His offspring' (*Acts* 17:24, 28).

Blessed is the Lord God of Israel, for He has visited and redeemed His people . . . to grant us that we, being delivered from the hand of our enemies, might serve Him without fear, in holiness and righteousness before Him all the days of our life (*Luke* 1:68, 74–75).

The commandments can be regarded as ten protecting friends. What an asset! Ten friends to guard our ways. They go with us into every activity and follow us into every interest. Ten watchmen of our path – these are the Ten Commandments of God. He has set them around us for our sakes because he loves us.

It is important to understand that there is a positive and a negative side to each commandment. The positive side expresses the duties which are commanded; the negative side expresses the sins which are forbidden. In all that follows we are indebted to the helpful instruction given in the *Larger Catechism* of the Westminster Assembly.

Duties Required in the First Commandment

The duty to know and acknowledge God to be the only true God:

'As for you, my son Solomon, know the God of your father, and serve Him with a loyal heart and with a willing mind; for the Lord searches all hearts and understands all the intent of the thoughts. If you seek Him, He will be found by you; but if you forsake Him, He will cast you off forever' (*1 Chron.* 28:9; See also *2 Kings* 20:3; *2 Chron.* 15:2; *Deut.* 31:17).

Are there any among the idols of the nations that can cause rain ?
Or can the heavens give showers ?
Are You not He, O Lord our God?
Therefore we will wait for You,
Since You have made all these (*Jer.* 14:22).

The duty to worship God:

Oh come, let us worship and bow down;
Let us kneel before the LORD our Maker.
For He *is* our God,
And we *are* the people of His pasture,
And the sheep of His hand (*Psa. 95: 6–7*).

(See also *Phil. 2:10; Psa. 79:13*)

The duty to glorify God:

Give unto the LORD the glory due to His name;
Worship the LORD in the beauty of holiness (*Psa. 29:2*).

The duty to think about God:

Then those who feared the LORD spoke to one another,
And the Lord listened and heard *them*;
So a book of remembrance was written before Him
For those who fear the LORD
And who meditate on His name (*Mal. 3:16*).

The duty to meditate on God:

When I remember You on my bed,
I meditate on You in the *night* watches (*Psa. 63:6*).

(See also *Psa. 42:8*)

The duty to remember God:

Remember now your Creator in the days of your youth,
Before the difficult days come,
And the years draw near when you say,
'I have no pleasure in them' (*Eccles. 12:1*).

The duty to honour God:

'A son honors *his* father,
And a servant *his* master.
If then I am the Father,
Where *is* My honor?

[14]

And if I *am* a Master,
Where *is* My reverence?'
Says the Lord of hosts
To you priests who despise My name.
Yet you say, 'In what way have we despised Your name?'
(*Mal.* 1:6).

(*See also* Luke 6:46)

The duty to esteem God highly:

Also Your righteousness, O God, *is* very high,
You who have done great things;
O God, who is like You? (*Psa.* 71:19)

The duty to believe God:

Thus Israel saw the great work which the LORD had done in
Egypt; so the people feared the LORD, and believed the LORD
and His servant Moses (*Exod.* 14:31).

The duty to trust God:

Trust in the Lord forever,
For in YAH, the LORD, *is* everlasting strength (*Isa.* 26:4).

The duty to delight in God:

Delight yourself also in the LORD,
And He shall give you the desires of your heart (*Psa.* 37:4).

The duty to rejoice in God:

Be glad in the LORD and rejoice, you righteous;
And shout for joy, all *you* upright in heart! (*Psa.* 32:11).

The duty to obey God and submit to him:

'But this is what I commanded them, saying, "Obey My
voice, and I will be your God, and you shall be My people.
And walk in all the ways that I have commanded you, that
it may be well with you." ' (*Jer.* 7:23).

Therefore submit to God. Resist the devil and he will flee from you (*James* 4:7).

The duty to walk humbly before God:

He has shown you, O man, what *is* good;
And what does the LORD require of you
But to do justly,
To love mercy,
And to walk humbly with your God? (*Mic.* 6:8)

SINS FORBIDDEN IN THE FIRST COMMANDMENT

The sin of atheism:

The fool has said in his heart,
'*There is* no God.'
They are corrupt, they have done abominable works,
There is none who does good (*Psa.* 14:1).

Therefore remember . . . that at that time you were without Christ, being aliens from the commonwealth of Israel and strangers from the covenants of promise, having no hope and without God in the world (*Eph.* 2:11–12).

The sin of idolatry, having or worshipping more gods than one:

Saying to a tree, 'You *are* my father,'
And to a stone, 'You gave birth to me.'
For they have turned *their* back to Me, and not *their* face.
But in the time of their trouble
They will say, 'Arise and save us' (*Jer.* 2:27).

For they themselves declare concerning us what manner of entry we had to you, and how you turned to God from idols to serve the living and true God (*1 Thess.* 1:9).

The sin of omission or neglect of anything due to God:

'But you have not called upon Me, O Jacob;
And you have been weary of Me, O Israel.

You have not brought Me the sheep for your burnt offerings,
Nor have you honored Me with your sacrifices.
I have not caused you to serve with grain offerings,
Nor wearied you with incense.
You have bought Me no sweet cane with money,
Nor have you satisfied Me with the fat of your sacrifices;
But you have burdened Me with your sins,
You have wearied Me with your iniquities' (*Isa. 43:22–24*).

The sin of forgetting God:

Can a virgin forget her ornaments,
Or a bride her attire?
Yet My people have forgotten Me days without number (*Jer. 2:32*).

The sin of having false opinions about God:

To whom then will you liken God ?
Or what likeness will you compare to Him? (*Isa. 40:18*)

The sin of having unworthy and wicked thoughts about God:

These *things* you have done, and I kept silent;
You thought that I was altogether like you;
But I will rebuke you,
And set *them* in order before your eyes (*Psa. 50:21*).

The sin of curious searching into his secrets:

The secret *things belong* to the Lord our God, but those *things which are* revealed *belong* to us and to our children forever, that *we* may do all the words of this law (*Deut. 29:29*).

The sin of hatred of God:

Backbiters, haters of God, violent, proud, boasters, inventors of evil things, disobedient to parents (*Rom. 1:30*).

The sin of self–love:

For men will be lovers of themselves, lovers of money, boasters, proud, blasphemers, disobedient to parents, unthankful, unholy (*2 Tim.* 3:2).

The sin of self–seeking:

For all seek their own, not the things which are of Christ Jesus (*Phil.* 2:21).

The sin of inordinate and immoderate setting our mind, will, or affections upon things other than God:

Do not love the world or the things in the world. If anyone loves the world, the love of the Father is not in him. For all that *is* in the world–the lust of the flesh, the lust of the eyes, and the pride of life–is not of the Father but is of the world (*1 John* 2:15–16).

Set your mind on things above, not on things on the earth (*Col.* 3:2).

The sin of unbelief:

Beware, brethren, lest there be in any of you an evil heart of unbelief in departing from the living God (*Heb.* 3:12).

The sin of despair:

And Cain said to the LORD, 'My punishment *is* greater than I can bear!' (*Gen.* 4:13)

The sin of hardening our hearts:

But in accordance with your hardness and your impenitent heart you are treasuring up for yourself wrath in the day of wrath and revelation of the righteous judgment of of God (*Rom.* 2:5).

The sin of pride:

Hear and give ear:
Do not be proud,
For the LORD has spoken (*Jer.* 13:15).

The sin of tempting God:

> Jesus said to him, 'It is written again, *"You shall not tempt the Lord your God."'* (*Matt.* 4:7)

The sin of praying to or worshipping saints, angels, or any other creatures:

> My people ask counsel from their wooden *idols*,
> And their staff informs them.
> For the spirit of harlotry has caused *them* to stray,
> And they have played the harlot against their God (*Hos.* 4:12).

> As Peter was coming in, Cornelius met him and fell down at his feet and worshiped *him*. But Peter lifted him up, saying, 'Stand up; I myself am also a man' (*Acts* 10:25–26).

> Then the beast was captured, and with him the false prophet who worked signs in his presence, by which he deceived those who received the mark of the beast and those who worshiped his image. These two were cast alive into the lake of fire burning with brimstone (*Rev.* 19:20).

> Then Jesus said to him, 'Away with you, Satan! For it is written, *"You shall worship the Lord your God, and Him only you shall serve."'* (*Matt.* 4:10).

> Let no one cheat you of your reward, taking delight in *false* humility and worship of angels, intruding into those things which he has not seen, vainly puffed up by his fleshly mind (*Col.* 2:18).

The sin of all compacts and consulting with the devil:

> And the person who turns to mediums and familiar spirits, to prostitute himself with them, I will set My face against that person and cut him off from his people (*Lev.* 20:6).

The sin of making man the lord over our faith and conscience:

> Not that we have dominion over your faith, but are fellow

workers for your joy; for by faith you stand (2 Cor. 1:24).

For they bind heavy burdens, hard to bear, and lay *them* on men's shoulders; but they *themselves* will not move them with one of their fingers (*Matt.* 23:4).

The sin of resisting and grieving the Spirit:

You stiffnecked and uncircumcised in heart and ears! You always resist the Holy Spirit; as your fathers *did*, so *do* you (*Acts* 7:51).

And do not grieve the Holy Spirit of God, by whom you were sealed for the day of redemption (*Eph.* 4:30).

The sin of discontentment and impatience with God's dealings, thus charging him foolishly for the evils that he inflicts on us:

But as for me, my feet had almost stumbled;
My steps had nearly slipped.
For I *was* envious of the boastful,
When I saw the prosperity of the wicked . . .
Surely I have cleansed my heart *in* vain,
And washed my hands in innocence.
For all day long I have been plagued,
And chastened every morning.
If I had said, 'I will speak thus,'
Behold, I would have been untrue to the generation of Your children . . .
I *was* so foolish and ignorant;
I was *like* a beast before You (*Psa.* 73:2–3, 13–15, 22).

In all this Job did not sin nor charge God with wrong (*Job* 1:22).

These duties and sins found in the First Commandment should teach us to pray with the sweet psalmist of Israel (*Psa.* 119:5–8, 34–36, 47–48, 61–62, 77, 126, 142, 153, 165, 176):

The First Commandment

Oh, that my ways were directed
To keep Your statutes!
Then I would not be ashamed,
When I look into all Your commandments.
I will praise You with uprightness of heart,
When I learn Your righteous judgments.
I will keep Your statutes;
Oh, do not forsake me utterly! . . .
Give me understanding, and I shall keep Your law;
Indeed, I shall observe it with *my* whole heart.
Make me walk in the path of Your commandments,
For I delight in it.
Incline my heart to Your testimonies, and not to covetous-
ness . . .
And I will delight myself in Your commandments,
Which I love.
My hands also I will lift up to Your commandments,
Which I love,
And I will meditate on Your statutes . . .
The cords of the wicked have bound me,
But I have not forgotten Your law.
At midnight I will rise to give thanks to You,
Because of Your righteous judgments . . .
Let Your tender mercies come to me, that I may live;
For Your law *is* my delight . . .
It is time for *You* to act, O Lord,
For they have regarded Your law as void . . .
Your righteousness *is* an everlasting righteousness,
And Your law *is* truth . . .
Consider my affliction and deliver me,
For I do not forget Your law . . .
Great peace have those who love Your law,
And nothing causes them to stumble . . .
I have gone astray like a lost sheep;
Seek Your servant,
For I do not forget Your commandments.

The Second Commandment

*You shall not make for yourself a carved image –
any likeness of anything that is in heaven above,
or that is in the earth beneath, or that is in the
water under the earth; you shall not bow down to
them nor serve them. For I, the LORD your God,
am a jealous God, visiting the iniquity of the
fathers upon the children to the third and fourth
generations of those who hate Me, but showing
mercy to thousands, to those who love Me and
keep My commandments*
(Exod. 20:4–6).

Here is the second trusted, protecting friend, to guard our ways. It is going to guard our worship. For, you see, when we set about to worship God, all our sins and problems come to the fore to spoil that worship. Satan does not want us to worship the true God in a true way. Therefore, this commandment not only sets out what we are to refrain from in worshipping God, but it also directs our steps so that we will worship him in the way in which he wants to be worshipped. How would you summarize the

Second Commandment? What is the thrust of it? I believe it to be this: God wants to bind his people close to him in a union that leaves nothing between them. God wants to forge a close union with you and to let nothing separate you from him.

DUTIES REQUIRED IN THE SECOND COMMANDMENT

According to the *Larger Catechism*, the duties required in the Second Commandment are 'the receiving, observing, and keeping pure and entire, all such religious worship and ordinances as God hath instituted in his word; particularly prayer and thanksgiving in the name of Christ' (*Question* 108). The proof texts include Deuteronomy 32:46–47, where we read:

> 'And He said to them: "Set your hearts on all the words which I testify among you today, which you shall command your children to be careful to observe – all the words of this law. For it is not a futile thing for you, because it is your life, and by this word you shall prolong *your* days in the land which you cross over the Jordan to possess." '

The *Catechism* also cites the following Scriptures:

'Teaching them to observe all things that I have commanded you; and lo, I am with you always, *even* to the end of the age.' Amen (*Matt.* 28:20).

And they continued steadfastly in the apostles' doctrine and fellowship, in the breaking of bread, and in prayers (*Acts* 2:42).

I urge you in the sight of God who gives life to all things, and *before* Christ Jesus who witnessed the good confession before Pontius Pilate, that you keep this commandment without spot, blameless until our Lord Jesus Christ's appearing (*1 Tim.* 6:13–14).

Be anxious for nothing, but in everything by prayer and supplication, with thanksgiving, let your requests be made known to God (*Phil.* 4:6).

Giving thanks always for all things to God the Father in the name of our Lord Jesus Christ (*Eph.* 5:20).

Other duties required by this commandment include these:

The duty to read the Word:

Also it shall be, when he sits on the throne of his kingdom, that he shall write for himself a copy of this law in a book, from *the one* before the priests, the Levites. And it shall be with him, and he shall read it all the days of his life, that he may learn to fear the LORD his God and be careful to observe all the words of this law and these statutes (*Deut.* 17:18–19).

For Moses has had throughout many generations those who preach him in every city, being read in the synagogues every Sabbath (*Acts* 15:21).

The duty to hear the Word:

Therefore lay aside all filthiness and overflow of wickedness, and receive with meekness the implanted word, which is able to save your souls. But be doers of the word, and not hearers only, deceiving yourselves (*James* 1:21–22).

So I sent to you immediately, and you have done well to come. Now therefore, we are all present before God, to hear all the things commanded you by God (*Acts* 10:33).

The duty to administer and receive the sacraments:

Go therefore and make disciples of all the nations, baptizing them in the name of the Father and of the Son and of the Holy Spirit (*Matt.* 28:19).

For I received from the Lord that which I also delivered to you: that the Lord Jesus on the same night in which He was betrayed took bread; and when He had given thanks, He broke it and said, 'Take, eat; this is My body which is broken for you; do this in remembrance of Me.' In the same manner *He* also *took* the cup after supper, saying, 'This cup is the new covenant in My blood. This do, as often as you drink it, in remembrance of Me.' For as often as you eat this bread and drink this cup, you proclaim the Lord's death till He comes (*1 Cor.* 11:23–26).

The duty of church government and discipline:

Moreover if your brother sins against you, go and tell him his fault between you and him alone. If he hears you, you have gained your brother. But if he will not hear, take with you one or two more, that 'by the mouth of two or three witnesses every word may be established.' And if he refuses to hear them, tell it to the church. But if he refuses even to hear the church, let him be to you like a heathen and a tax collector (*Matt.* 18:15–17).

And I will give you the keys of the kingdom of heaven, and whatever you bind on earth will be bound in heaven, and whatever you loose on earth will be loosed in heaven (*Matt.* 16:19).

And God has appointed these in the church: first apostles, second prophets, third teachers, after that miracles, then gifts of healings, helps, administrations, varieties of tongues (*1 Cor.* 12:28).

The duty to receive and maintain the ministry:

And He Himself gave some *to be* apostles, some prophets, some evangelists, and some pastors and teachers, for the equipping of the saints for the work of ministry, for the edifying of the body of Christ (*Eph.* 4:11–12).

Let the elders who rule well be counted worthy of double honor, especially those who labor in the word and doctrine. For the Scripture says, '*You shall not muzzle an ox while it treads out the grain,*' and, 'The laborer is worthy of his wages.' (*1 Tim.* 5:17–18).

Who ever goes to war at his own expense? Who plants a vineyard and does not eat of its fruit? Or who tends a flock and does not drink of the milk of the flock? Do I say these things as a *mere* man? Or does not the law say the same also? For it is written in the law of Moses, '*You shall not muzzle an ox while it treads out the grain.*' Is it oxen God is concerned about? Or does He say *it* altogether for our sakes? For our sakes, no doubt, *this* is written, that he who plows should plow in hope, and he who threshes in hope should be partaker of his hope. If we have sown spiritual things for you, *is it* a great thing if we reap your material things ? If others are partakers of *this* right over you, *are* we not even more? Nevertheless we have not used this right, but endure all things lest we hinder the gospel of Christ. Do you not know that those who minister the holy things eat *of the things* of the temple, and those who serve at the altar partake of *the offerings of* the altar? Even so the Lord has commanded that those who preach the gospel should live from the gospel (*1 Cor. 9:7–15*).

The duty of religious fasting:

'Now, therefore,' says the LORD,
'Turn to Me with all your heart,
With fasting, with weeping, and with mourning.'
(*Joel* 2:12).

Do not deprive one another except with consent for a time, that you may give yourselves to fasting and prayer; and come together again so that Satan does not tempt you because of your lack of self-control (*1 Cor. 7:5*).

The duty to disapprove of, detest and oppose all false worship:

Now while Paul waited for them at Athens, his spirit was provoked within him when he saw that the city was given over to idols. Therefore he reasoned in the synagogue with the Jews and with the *Gentile* worshipers, and in the marketplace daily with those who happened to be there (*Acts* 17:16–17).

Their sorrows shall be multiplied who hasten *after* another *god*;
Their drink offerings of blood I will not offer,
Nor take up their names on my lips (*Psa.* 16:4).

SINS FORBIDDEN IN THE SECOND COMMANDMENT

The sin of enticing to idolatry:

If your brother, the son of your mother, your son or your daughter, the wife of your bosom, or your friend who is as your own soul, secretly entices you, saying, 'Let us go and serve other gods,' which you have not known, neither you nor your fathers, of the gods of the people which are all around you, near to you or far off from you, from one end of the earth to the *other* end of the earth, you shall not consent to him or listen to him, nor shall your eye pity him, nor shall you spare him or conceal him (*Deut.* 13:6–8).

The sin of approving any religious worship not instituted by God himself:

Take heed to yourself that you are not ensnared to follow them, after they are destroyed from before you, and that you do not inquire after their gods, saying, 'How did these nations serve their gods? I also will do likewise.' You shall not worship the LORD your God in that way; for every abomination to the LORD which He hates they have done to their gods; for they burn even their sons and daughters in the fire to their gods. Whatever I command you, be careful to observe it; you shall not add to it nor take away from it (*Deut.* 12:30–32).

The sin of tolerating false religion:

'It shall be in that day,' says the LORD of hosts, '*that* I will cut off the names of the idols from the land, and they shall no longer be remembered. I will also cause the prophets and the unclean spirit to depart from the land. It shall come to pass *that* if anyone still prophesies, then his father and mother who begot him will say to him, 'You shall not live, because you have spoken lies in the name of the LORD.' And his father and mother who begot him shall thrust him through when he prophesies (*Zech*. 13:2–3).

I know your works, your labor, your patience, and that you cannot bear those who are evil. And you have tested those who say they are apostles and are not, and have found them liars . . . But I have a few things against you, because you have there those who hold the doctrine of Balaam, who taught Balak to put a stumbling block before the children of Israel, to eat things sacrificed to idols, and to commit sexual immorality. Thus you also have those who hold the doctrine of the Nicolaitans, which thing I hate . . . Nevertheless I have a few things against you, because you allow that woman Jezebel, who calls herself a prophetess, to teach and seduce My servants to commit sexual immorality and eat things sacrificed to idols (*Rev*. 2:2, 14–15, 20).

The sin of making any representation of God, of all or of any of the Three Persons, either inwardly in our mind or outwardly in any kind of image or likeness of any creature:

Take careful heed to yourselves, for you saw no form when the LORD spoke to you at Horeb out of the midst of the fire, lest you act corruptly and make for yourselves a carved image in the form of any figure: the likeness of male or female, the likeness of any animal that is on the earth or the likeness of any winged bird that flies in the air, the likeness of anything that creeps on the ground or the likeness of any fish that is in the water beneath the earth. And *take heed*, lest you lift your eyes to heaven, and *when* you see the sun, the moon, and the stars, all the host of heaven, you feel driven to worship them and serve them, which the LORD your God has given to all the peoples under the whole heaven as a heritage (*Deut*. 4:15–19).

Therefore, since we are the offspring of God, we ought not to think that the Divine Nature is like gold or silver or stone, something shaped by art and man's devising (*Acts* 17:29).

Because, although they knew God, they did not glorify *Him* as God, nor were thankful, but became futile in their thoughts, and their foolish hearts were darkened. Professing to be wise, they became fools, and changed the glory of the incorruptible God into an image made like corruptible man–and birds and four-footed animals and creeping things (*Rom.* 1:21–23).

Who exchanged the truth of God for the lie, and worshiped and served the creature rather than the Creator, who is blessed forever. Amen (*Rom.* 1:25).

The sin of worshipping images:

But if not, let it be known to you, O king, that we do not serve your gods, nor will we worship the gold image which you have set up (*Dan.* 3:18).

But then, indeed, when you did not know God, you served those which by nature are not gods (*Gal.* 4:8).

The sin of making any representation of imagined deities:

They have turned aside quickly out of the way which I commanded them. They have made themselves a molded calf, and worshiped it and sacrificed to it, and said, 'This *is* your god, O Israel, that brought you out of the land of Egypt!' (*Exod.* 32:8)

The sin of worshipping or serving imagined deities:

So they took the bull which was given them, and they prepared *it*, and called on the name of Baal from morning even till noon, saying, 'O Baal, hear us!' But *there was* no voice; no one answered. Then they leaped about the altar which they had made . . . So they cried aloud, and cut themselves, as was their custom, with knives and lances, until the blood gushed out on them (*1 Kings* 18:26, 28).

But you *are* those who forsake the LORD,
Who forget My holy mountain,
Who prepare a table for Gad,
And who furnish a drink offering for Meni (*Isa.* 65:11).

The sin of superstition:

'Do not touch, do not taste, do not handle,' which all concern things which perish with the using–according to the commandments and doctrines of men? These things indeed have an appearance of wisdom in self-imposed religion, *false* humility, and neglect of the body, *but are* of no value against the indulgence of the flesh (*Col.* 2:21–23).

The sin of corrupting the worship of God:

You offer defiled food on My altar.
But say,
'In what way have we defiled You?'
By saying,
'The table of the LORD is contemptible.'
And when you offer the blind as a sacrifice,
Is it not evil?
And when you offer the lame and sick,
Is it not evil?
Offer it then to your governor!
Would he be pleased with you?
Would he accept you favorably?
Says the LORD of hosts (*Mal.* 1:7– 8).

The sin of adding to or taking away from the worship of God:

You shall not add to the word which I command you, nor take from it, that you may keep the commandments of the LORD your God which I command you (*Deut.* 4:2).

And in vain they worship Me, teaching as doctrines the commandments of men (*Matt.* 15:9).

The sin of simony:

And when Simon saw that through the laying on of the apostles' hands the Holy Spirit was given, he offered them money (*Acts* 8:18).

The sin of sacrilege:

You who say, 'Do not commit adultery,' do you commit adultery? You who abhor idols, do you rob temples? (*Rom.* 2:22).

Will a man rob God ?
Yet you have robbed Me!
But you say,
'In what way have we robbed You?'
In tithes and offerings (*Mal.* 3:8).

The sin of despising the worship and ordinances of God:

But they made light of it and went their ways, one to his own farm, another to his business (*Matt.* 22:5).

You also say,
'Oh, what a weariness!'
And you sneer at it . . . (*Mal.* 1:13).

The sin of hindering and opposing the worship and ordinances of God:

But woe to you, scribes and Pharisees, hypocrites! For you shut up the kingdom of heaven against men; for you neither go in *yourselves*, nor do you allow those who are entering to go in (*Matt.* 23:13).

On the next Sabbath almost the whole city came together to hear the word of God. But when the Jews saw the multitudes, they were filled with envy; and contradicting and blaspheming, they opposed the things spoken by Paul (*Acts*. 13:44–45).

Who killed both the Lord Jesus and their own prophets, and have persecuted us; and they do not please God and are contrary to all men, forbidding us to speak to the Gentiles that they may be saved, so as always to fill up *the measure of* their sins; but wrath has come upon them to the uttermost (*1 Thess.* 2:15–16).

Reasons attached to the Second Commandment to reinforce it:

These words are added to the Second Commandment:

'For I, the LORD your God, am a jealous God, visiting the iniquity of the fathers on the children to the third and fourth generations of those who hate Me, but showing mercy to thousands, to those who love Me and keep My commandments' (*Exod.* 20:5–6).

These words teach us:

1. *God's sovereignty over and ownership of us:*

So the King will greatly desire your beauty;
Because He *is* your Lord, worship Him (*Psa.* 45:11).

They sing the song of Moses, the servant of God, and the song of the Lamb, saying: 'Great and marvelous are Your works, Lord God Almighty! Just and true are Your ways, O King of the saints! Who shall not fear You, O Lord, and glorify Your name? For *You* alone *are* holy. For all nations shall come and worship before You, For Your judgments have been manifested' (*Rev.* 15:3–4).

2. *The zeal of God for His own worship:*

But you shall destroy their altars, break their *sacred* pillars, and cut down their wooden images (for you shall worship no other god, for the LORD, whose name is Jealous, is a jealous God) (*Exod.* 34:13–14).

[32]

3. *God's indignation against all false worship:*

Rather, that the things which the Gentiles sacrifice they sacrifice to demons and not to God, and I do not want you to have fellowship with demons. You cannot drink the cup of the Lord and the cup of demons; you cannot partake of the Lord's table and of the table of demons. Or do we provoke the Lord to jealousy? Are we stronger than He? (*1 Cor.* 10:20–22).

'The children gather wood, the fathers kindle the fire, and the women knead dough, to make cakes for the queen of heaven; and *they* pour out drink offerings to other gods, that they may provoke Me to anger. Do they provoke Me to anger?' says the LORD. 'Do *they* not *provoke* themselves, to the shame of their own faces?' Therefore thus says the Lord GOD: 'Behold, My anger and My fury will be poured out on this place—on man and on beast, on the trees of the field and on the fruit of the ground. And it will burn and not be quenched' (*Jer.* 7:18–20).

They provoked Him to jealousy with foreign *gods*;
With abominations they provoked Him to anger.
They sacrificed to demons, not to God,
To gods they did not know,
To new *gods*, new arrivals
That your fathers did not fear.
Of the Rock *who* begot you, you are unmindful,
And have forgotten the God who fathered you.
And when the Lord saw *it*, He spurned them,
Because of the provocation of His sons and His daughters.
And He said: 'I will hide My face from them,
I will see what their end *will be*,
For they *are* a perverse generation,
Children in whom *is* no faith' (*Deut.* 32:16–20).

4. *His promise of endless blessing to those who love him and keep his commandments:*

> Oh, that they had such a heart in them that they would fear Me and always keep all My commandments, that it might be well with them and with their children forever! (*Deut.* 5:29)

The Third Commandment

You shall not take the name of the LORD your God in vain, for the LORD will not hold him guiltless who takes His name in vain (Exod. 20:7).

Nobody knows your name unless you tell it to him or he finds out from someone else. When you tell someone your name, you have made a gift to him. In truth, however, human names, in comparison with the import of God's names, are fairly insubstantial and insignificant.

When God tells us his name, something of tremendous significance happens. Think how great it is: God came out of nameless, unapproachable majesty into our realm and gave us his name. When he gave the commandments, he said, '*I am Jehovah thy God. I am the LORD thy God*'. Think what a marvellous thing that is! He gave us a gift, an insight.

DUTIES REQUIRED IN THE THIRD COMMANDMENT

According to the *Larger Catechism*, the Third Commandment requires 'that the name of God, his titles, attributes, ordinances, the word, sacraments, prayer, oaths, vows, lots, his works, and whatsoever else there is whereby he makes himself known, be holily and reverently used in thought, meditation, word, and writing; by an holy profession, and answerable conversation, to the glory of God, and the good of ourselves, and others' (*Question* 112).

We can single out the following requirements of the Third Commandment:

The duty to use God's Name holily and reverently:

1. In thought and meditation:

Then those who feared the LORD spoke to one another,
And the LORD listened and heard *them*;
So a book of remembrance was written before Him
For those who fear the LORD
And who meditate on His name (*Mal.* 3:16).

O LORD, our Lord,
How excellent *is* Your name in all the earth,
Who have set Your glory above the heavens! . . .
When I consider Your heavens, the work of Your fingers,
The moon and the stars, which You have ordained,
What is man that You are mindful of him,
And the son of man that You visit him? . . .
O LORD, our Lord,
How excellent *is* Your name in all the earth!
(*Psa.* 8:1, 3–4, 9)

2. In word:

And *whatever* you do in word or deed, *do* all in the name of the Lord Jesus, giving thanks to God the Father through Him (*Col.* 3:17).

Sing to Him, sing psalms to Him;
Talk of all His wondrous works! . . .

Remember His marvelous works which He has done,
His wonders, and the judgments of His mouth
(*Psa.* 105:2, 5).

3. *In writing:*

This will be written for the generation to come,
That a people yet to be created may praise the LORD
(*Psa.* 102:18).

4. *In holy profession and conversation:*

But sanctify the Lord God in your hearts, and always *be*
ready to *give* a defense to everyone who asks you a reason
for the hope that is in you, with meekness and fear (*1 Pet.*
3:15).

For all people walk each in the name of his god,
But we will walk in the name of the LORD our God
Forever and ever (*Mic.* 4:5).

Only let your conduct be worthy of the gospel of Christ, so
that whether I come and see you or am absent, I may hear of
your affairs, that you stand fast in one spirit, with one mind
striving together for the faith of the gospel (*Phil.* 1:27).

SINS FORBIDDEN IN THE THIRD COMMANDMENT

The sin of not using God's Name as we ought:

'If you will not hear,
And if you will not take *it* to heart,
To give glory to My name,'
Says the LORD of hosts,
'I will send a curse upon you,
And I will curse your blessings.
Yes, I have cursed them already,
Because you do not take it to heart' (*Mal.* 2:2).

The sin of using God's Name in an ignorant way:

For as I was passing through and considering the objects of your worship, I even found an altar with this inscription:

TO THE UNKNOWN GOD

Therefore, the One whom you worship without knowing, Him I proclaim to you (*Acts* 17:23).

The sin of using God's Name in a vain, irreverent, or profane way:

Lest I be full and deny *You*,
And say, 'Who *is* the LORD?'
Or lest I be poor and steal,
And profane the name of my God (*Prov.* 30:9).

The sin of using God's Name in a superstitious and presumptuous way:

And when the people had come into the camp, the elders of Israel said, 'Why has the Lord defeated us today before the Philistines? Let us bring the ark of the covenant of the Lord from Shiloh to us, that when it comes among us it may save us from the hand of our enemies.' So the people sent to Shiloh, that they might bring from there the ark of the covenant of the LORD of hosts, who dwells *between* the cherubim. And the two sons of Eli, Hophni and Phinehas, *were* there with the ark of the covenant of God. And when the ark of the covenant of the LORD came into the camp, all Israel shouted so loudly that the earth shook (*1 Sam.* 4:3–5).

The sin of mentioning his titles, attributes or ordinances blasphemously:

Nor let Hezekiah make you trust in the LORD, saying, 'The LORD will surely deliver us; this city shall not be given into the hand of the king of Assyria.' . . . But do not listen to Hezekiah, lest he persuade you, saying, 'The LORD will deliver us.' Has any of the gods of the nations at all delivered its land from the hand of the king of Assyria?

Where *are* the gods of Hamath and Arpad? Where *are* the gods of Sepharvaim and Hena and Ivah? Indeed, have they delivered Samaria from my hand? Who among all the gods of the lands have delivered their countries from my hand, that the LORD should deliver Jerusalem from my hand? (*2 Kings* 18:30, 32–35)

Whom have you reproached and blasphemed? Against whom have you raised *your* voice, and lifted up your eyes on high? Against the Holy *One* of Israel (*2 Kings* 19:22).

And Pharaoh said, 'Who is the LORD, that I should obey His voice to let Israel go? I do not know the LORD, nor will I let Israel go' (*Exod.* 5:2).

For they speak against You wickedly;
Your enemies take *Your name* in vain (*Psa.* 139:20).

But to the wicked God says:
'What *right* have you to declare My statutes,
Or take My covenant in your mouth,
Seeing you hate instruction
And cast My words behind you?' (*Psa.* 50:16, 17)

The sin of wicked cursing, vows and oaths:

Now when King David came to Bahurim, there was a man from the family of the house of Saul, whose name *was* Shimei the son of Gera, coming from there. He came out, cursing continously as he came (*2 Sam.* 16:5).

How shall I pardon you for this?
Your children have forsaken Me
And sworn by *those that are* not gods (*Jer.* 5:7).

You shall not bring the wages of a harlot or the price of a dog to the house of the LORD your God for any vowed offering, for both of these *are* an abomination to the LORD your God (*Deut.* 23:18).

And when it was day, some of the Jews banded together and bound themselves under an oath, saying that they would neither eat nor drink till they had killed Paul (*Acts* 23:12).

The sin of misapplying God's decrees and providences:

But if our unrighteousness demonstrates the righteousness of God, what shall we say? *Is* God unjust who inflicts wrath? (I speak as a man.) Certainly not! For then how will God judge the world? For if the truth of God has increased through my lie to His glory, why am I also still judged as a sinner? (*Rom.* 3:5–7)

Because the sentence against an evil work is not executed speedily, therefore the heart of the sons of men is fully set in them to do evil (*Eccles.* 8:11).

This *is* an evil in all that is done under the sun: that one thing *happens* to all. Truly the hearts of the sons of men are full of evil; madness *is* in their hearts while they live, and after that *they go* to the dead (*Eccles.* 9:3).

The sin of misinterpreting, misapplying, or in any way perverting the Word of God:

Because with lies you have made the heart of the righteous sad, whom I have not made sad; and you have strengthened the hands of the wicked, so that he does not turn from his wicked way to save his life (*Ezek.* 13:22).

As also in all his epistles, speaking in them of these things, in which are some things hard to understand, which untaught and unstable *people* twist to their own destruction, as *they do* also the rest of the Scriptures (*2 Pet.* 3:16).

Teacher, Moses said that if a man dies, having no children, his brother shall marry his wife and raise up offspring for his brother. Now there were with us seven brothers. The first died after he had married, and having no offspring, left his wife to his brother. Likewise the second also, and the third, even to the seventh. Last of all the woman died also. Therefore, in the resurrection, whose wife of the seven will she be? For they all had her.' Jesus answered and said to them, 'You are mistaken, not knowing the Scriptures nor the power of God. For in the resurrection they neither marry nor are given in marriage, but are like angels of God in heaven.' (*Matt.* 22:24–30).

The sin of making profession of religion in hypocrisy or for underhand ends:

Having a form of godliness but denying its power. And from such people turn away! (*2 Tim.* 3:5)

Woe to you, scribes and Pharisees, hypocrites! For you devour widows' houses, and for a pretense make long prayers. Therefore you will receive greater condemnation (*Matt.* 23:14).

Take heed that you do not do your charitable deeds before men, to be seen by them. Otherwise you have no reward from your Father in heaven. Therefore, when you do a charitable deed, do not sound a trumpet before you as the hypocrites do in the synagogues and in the streets, that they may have glory from men. Assuredly, I say to you, they have their reward . . . And when you pray, you shall not be like the hypocrites. For they love to pray standing in the synagogues and on the corners of the streets, that they may be seen by men. Assuredly, I say to you, they have their reward . . . Moreover, when you fast, do not be like the hypocrites, with a sad countenance. For they disfigure their faces that they may appear to men to be fasting. Assuredly, I say to you, they have their reward (*Matt.* 6:1–2, 5, 16).

The Fourth Commandment

Remember the Sabbath day, to keep it holy.
Six days you shall labor and do all your work,
but the seventh day is the Sabbath of the LORD
your God. In it you shall do no work: you, nor
your son, nor your daughter, nor your male
servant, nor your female servant, nor your cattle,
nor your stranger who is within your gates.
For in six days the LORD *made the heavens and*
the earth, the sea and all that is in them,
and rested the seventh day. Therefore the LORD
blessed the Sabbath day and hallowed it
(Exod. 20:8–11).

Teachers, preachers, theologians and ordinary Christians differ more on the interpretation and application of this commandment than on that of any of the other nine, and for that reason we will give more space to a consideration of it. We must remember that, in spite of the differences in detailed application, it is still one of the Ten Commandments.

The Sabbath is a sign of God's covenant with his people:

> Speak also to the children of Israel, saying: 'Surely My Sabbaths you shall keep, for it *is* a sign between Me and you throughout your generations, that *you* may know that I *am* the LORD who sanctifies you' (*Exod.* 31:13).

> You shall keep My Sabbaths and reverence My sanctuary: I *am* the LORD' (*Lev.* 19:30).

It is to be a delight:

> 'If you turn away your foot from the Sabbath,
> *From* doing your pleasure on My holy day,
> And call the Sabbath a delight,
> The holy *day* of the LORD honorable,
> And shall honor Him, not doing your own ways,
> Nor finding your own pleasure,
> Nor speaking *your own* words,
> Then you shall delight yourself in the LORD;
> And I will cause you to ride on the high hills of the earth,
> And feed you with the heritage of Jacob your father.
> The mouth of the LORD has spoken' (*Isa.* 58:13–14).

It has also been called the Queen Day of the week and God's Harvest Day because more of his truth goes out and more fruit is gathered in to his glory on this day than on any other day. The Puritans called it the market day of the soul; a day for entering the very suburbs of heaven.

The Character of the Fourth Commandment

'The Sabbath,' wrote Matthew Henry, 'is a sacred and divine institution; but we must receive and embrace it as a privilege and a benefit, not as a task and a drudgery. First, God never designed it to be an imposition upon us, and therefore we must not make it so to ourselves . . . Secondly, God did design it to be an advantage to us, and so we must make and improve it . . . He had some regard to our bodies in the institution, that they might rest . . . He had much more regard for our souls. The Sabbath was made a day of rest, only in order to its being a day of holy work, a day of communion with God, a day of praise and thanksgiving; and the rest from worldly business is therefore necessary, that we may closely apply ourselves to this work, and spend the whole time in it, in public and private . . . See here what a good master we serve, all whose institutions are for our own benefit . . .' (*Commentary on the Whole Bible*, notes on Mark 1:17).

This quotation fairly sums up the Puritan approach to the Lord's Day. Here we would merely underline three of Henry's points and add a fourth by way of corollary.

1. Sabbath-keeping means action, not inaction. The Lord's Day is not a day of idleness. 'Idleness is a sin every day but much more on the Lord's Day' (J. Dod, *On the Commandments*, p. 143). We do not keep the Sabbath holy by lounging around doing nothing. We are to rest from the business of our earthly calling in order to prosecute the business of our heavenly calling. If we do not spend the day doing the latter, we fail to keep it holy.

2. Sabbath-keeping is not a tedious burden, but a joyful privilege. The Sabbath is not a fast, but a feast, a day for rejoicing in the works of a gracious God, and joy may be its temper throughout. 'Joy suits no person so much as a saint, and it becomes no season so well as a Sabbath' (George Swinnock, *Works*, Vol. 1, Edinburgh: Banner of Truth Trust, 1992, p. 239). 'It is the duty and glory of a Christian to rejoice in the Lord every day, but especially on the Lord's day . . . To fast on the Lord's day, saith Ignatius, is to kill Christ; but to rejoice in the Lord on this day, and to rejoice in all the duties of this day . . . this is to crown Christ, this is to lift up Christ' (Thomas Brooks, *Works,* Vol. 6, Edinburgh: Banner of Truth Trust, 1980, p. 299). Joy must be the keynote of public worship. Baxter, in particular, deplores drab, mournful services. There must be no gloom on the Lord's Day. And those who say that they cannot find

joy in the spiritual exercises of a Christian Sunday thereby show that there is something very wrong with them.

3. Sabbath-keeping is not a useless labour, but a means of grace. 'God hath made it our duty, by his institution, to set apart this day for a special seeking of his grace and blessing, from which we may argue that he will be especially ready to confer his grace on those who thus seek it . . . The sabbath-day is an accepted time, a day of salvation, a time wherein God especially loves to be sought and loves to be found. . .' (Jonathan Edwards, *Works*, Vol. 2, Edinburgh: Banner of Truth Trust, 1974, p. 102).

4. Sabbath-breaking brings chastisement, as does the abuse of any God-given privilege and means of grace. Spiritual decline and material loss accrue to both individuals and communities for this sin. The good gifts of God may not be despised with impunity. Thomas Fuller thought that the Civil War, and Brooks that the fire of London, came as judgment on the nation for Sabbath-breaking.

I want to say just a word about the changing of the Jewish Sabbath to the Lord's Day. Let me use the words of Thomas Watson:

> The grand reason for changing the Jewish Sabbath to the Lord's Day is that it puts us in mind of the 'Mystery of our redemption by Christ.' The reason why God instituted the old Sabbath was to be a memorial of the creation; but he has now brought the first day of the week in its room in memory of a more glorious work than creation, which is redemption. Great was the work of creation, but greater was the work of redemption. As it was said, 'The glory of this latter house shall be greater than of the former' (*Hag.* 2:9). So the glory of the redemption was greater than the glory of the creation. Great wisdom was seen in making us, but more miraculous wisdom in saving us. Great power was seen in bringing us out of nothing, but greater power in helping us when we were worse than nothing. It cost more to redeem than to

create us. In creation it was but speaking a word (*Psa.* 48:5); in redeeming there was shedding of blood (*1 Pet.* 1:19). Creation was the work of God's fingers (*Psa.* 8:3), redemption was the work of his arm (*Luke* 1:51). In creation, God gave us ourselves; in the redemption, he gave us himself. By creation, we have life in Adam; by redemption, we have life in Christ (*Col.* 3:3). By creation, we had a right to an earthly paradise: by redemption, we have a title to a heavenly kingdom. Christ might well change the seventh day of the week into the first, as it puts us in mind of our redemption, which is a more glorious work than creation (*The Ten Commandments*, London: Banner of Truth Trust, 1959, p. 96).

Our generation is in desperate need of some biblical instruction concerning the Fourth Commandment. We should be shocked when we learn that some Bible teachers and ministers undermine the practice of the worship and service of God by excluding the Fourth Commandment from the Decalogue. Antinomians rant against the Fourth Commandment. Legalists make it unpleasant and unpalatable. Instructed Christians delight in it. The Fourth Commandment is worthy of serious study because of its importance in our spiritual warfare and is critical for our corrupt generation.

The Fourth Commandment is an integral part of the first table of the law, which deals systematically with our love to God, who is the object of our worship:

1. The First Commandment shows us that love to God requires our exclusive worship of him and service to him.

2. The Second Commandment teaches us the manner in which love will express itself in worship and service to God.

3. The Third Commandment teaches us the attitude of reverence which love will bring to God's worship and service.

4. The Fourth Commandment instructs us what time is required to express our love in worship.

So long as we are creatures of time, we who love must devote time to him who is the object of our supreme love.

Every rule of ethics can be misused and made to sound absurd or complicated by bringing to it a host of questions about its application. It is a favourite practice of those who oppose any moral law to raise extremely difficult circumstances in which application to moral conduct seems unmanageable or in which one principle appears to be in conflict with another. In this way the moral standard is declared absurd. The Fourth Commandment is not exempt from this kind of treatment. It is important that before you are dazzled with the complexities of supposed difficulties, you examine the simplicity and practicality of this commandment.

DUTIES REQUIRED IN THE FOURTH COMMANDMENT

The answer to Question 116 in the *Larger Catechism* gives us an overall picture of what is required in the Fourth Commandment.

> The fourth commandment requireth of all men the sanctifying, or keeping holy to God such set times as he hath appointed in his word, expressly one whole day in seven; which was the seventh from the beginning of the world to the resurrection of Christ, and the first day of the week ever since, and so to continue to the end of the world; which is the Christian sabbath, and in the New Testament called *The Lord's Day*.

The duty of resting from employments which would be lawful on other days:

> Then Moses said, 'Eat that [manna] today, for today *is* a Sabbath to the LORD; today you will not find it in the field. Six days you shall gather it, but on the seventh day, the Sabbath, there will be none.' Now it happened *that some* of the people went out on the seventh day to gather, but they found none. And the LORD said to Moses, 'How long do you

refuse to keep My commandments and My laws?' (*Exod.* 16:25–28).

Thus says the LORD: 'Take heed to yourselves, and bear no burden on the Sabbath day, nor bring *it* in by the gates of Jerusalem; nor carry a burden out of your houses on the Sabbath day, nor do any work, but hallow the Sabbath day, as I commanded your fathers' (*Jer.* 17:21–22).

The duty of public and private worship:

If you turn away your foot from the Sabbath,
From doing your pleasure on My holy day,
And call the Sabbath a delight,
The holy *day* of the LORD honorable,
And shall honor Him, not doing your own ways,
Nor finding your own pleasure,
Nor speaking *your own* words,
Then you shall delight yourself in the LORD;
And I will cause you to ride on the high hills of the earth,
And feed you with the heritage of Jacob your father.
The mouth of the LORD has spoken (*Isa.* 58:13–14).

So He came to Nazareth, where He had been brought up. And as His custom was, He went into the synagogue on the Sabbath day, and stood up to read (*Luke* 4:16).

Now on the first day of the week, when the disciples came together to break bread, Paul, ready to depart the next day, spoke to them and continued his message until midnight (*Acts* 20:7).

Now concerning the collection for the saints, as I have given orders to the churches of Galatia, so you must do also: on the first *day* of the week let each one of you lay something aside, storing up as he may prosper, that there be no collections when I come (*1 Cor. 16:1–2*).

'And it shall come to pass
That from one New Moon to another,
And from one Sabbath to another,

All flesh shall come to worship before Me,' says the LORD (*Isa.* 66:23).

SINS FORBIDDEN IN THE FOURTH COMMANDMENT

The sin of omitting duties:

Her priests have violated My law and profaned My holy things; they have not distinguished between the holy and unholy, nor have they made known the *difference* between the unclean and the clean; and they have hidden their eyes from My Sabbaths, so that I am profaned among them (*Ezek.* 22:26).

The sin of careless, negligent, unprofitable performing of duties:

So they come to you as people do, they sit before you *as* My people, and they hear your words, but they do not do them; for with their mouth they show much love, *but* their hearts pursue their *own* gain. Indeed you *are* to them as a very lovely song of one who has a pleasant voice and can play well on an instrument; for they hear your words, but they do not do them (*Ezek.* 33:31–32).

'When will the New Moon be past,
That we may sell grain?
And the Sabbath,
That we may trade wheat?
Making the ephah small and the shekel large,
Falsifying the scales by deceit . . . ' (*Amos* 8:5).

'You also say,
"Oh, what a weariness!"
And you sneer at it,'
Says the LORD of hosts.
'And you bring the stolen, the lame, and the sick;
Thus you bring an offering!
Should I accept this from your hand ?'
Says the LORD (*Mal.* 1:13).

The sin of profaning the day by idleness and doing what is in itself sinful:

Moreover they have done this to Me: they have defiled My sanctuary on the same day and profaned My Sabbaths (*Ezek.* 23:38).

The sin of all needless works and words:

'And it shall be, if you heed Me carefully,' says the LORD, 'to bring no burden through the gates of this city on the Sabbath day, but hallow the Sabbath day, to do no work in it, then shall enter the gates of this city kings and princes sitting on the throne of David, riding in chariots and on horses, they and their princes, accompanied by the men of Judah and the inhabitants of Jerusalem; and this city shall remain forever . . . But if you will not heed Me to hallow the Sabbath day, such as not carrying a burden when entering the gates of Jerusalem on the Sabbath day, then I will kindle a fire in its gates, and it shall devour the palaces of Jerusalem, and it shall not be quenched' (*Jer.* 17:24–25, 27).

'If you turn away your foot from the Sabbath,
From doing your pleasure on My holy day,
And call the Sabbath a delight,
The holy *day* of the LORD honorable,
And shall honor Him, not doing your own ways,
Nor finding your own pleasure,
Nor speaking *your own* words . . . (*Isa.* 58:13).

The *Larger Catechism* ends its exposition of the Fourth Commandment with two questions and answers. They are as follows:

What are the reasons annexed to the fourth commandment, the more to enforce it?

The reasons annexed to the fourth commandment, the more to enforce it, are taken from the equity of it, God allowing us six days of seven for our own affairs, and reserving but one for himself, in these words, *Six days shalt thou labour, and do all thy work:* from God's challenging a special propriety in that day, *The seventh day is the sabbath of the* LORD *thy God:* from the example of God, who *in six days made heaven and earth, the sea, and all that in them is, and rested the seventh day:* and from that blessing which God put upon that day, not only in sanctifying it to be a day for his service, but in ordaining it to be a means of blessing to us in our sanctifying it; *wherefore the* LORD *blessed the sabbath-day, and hallowed it.*

Why is the word 'Remember' set in the beginning of the fourth commandment?

The word *Remember* is set in the beginning of the fourth commandment, partly, because of the great benefit of remembering it, we being thereby helped in our preparation to keep it, and, in keeping it, better to keep all the rest of the commandments, and to continue a thankful remembrance of the two great benefits of creation and redemption, which contain a short abridgment of religion; and partly, because we are very ready to forget it, for that there is less light of nature for it, and yet it restraineth our natural liberty in things at other times lawful; that it cometh but once in seven days, and many worldly businesses come between, and too often take off our minds from thinking of it, either to prepare for it, or to sanctify it; and that Satan with his instruments much labour to blot out the glory, and even the memory of it, to bring in all irreligion and impiety.

John Newton, the great preacher and hymn writer, author of *Amazing Grace,* also wrote this hymn about the Sabbath, based on Isaiah 66:23. It seems fitting that we close this study with this wonderful hymn.

Safely through another week
God has brought us on our way;
Let us now a blessing seek,
Waiting in his courts today;

Day of all the week the best,
Emblem of eternal rest.

While we pray for pard'ning grace,
Through the dear Redeemer's Name,
Show thy reconciled face;
Take away our sin and shame;
From our worldly cares set free,
May we rest this day in thee.

Here we come thy Name to praise,
Let us feel thy presence near;
May thy glory meet our eyes,
While we in thy house appear:
Here afford us, Lord, a taste
Of our everlasting feast.

May thy gospel's joyful sound
Conquer sinners, comfort saints;
May the fruits of grace abound,
Bring relief for all complaints:
Thus may all our Sabbaths prove,
Till we join the church above.

The Fifth Commandment

Honor your father and your mother, that your days may be long upon the land which the LORD your God is giving you
(Exod. 20:12).

T he first four commandments, as we have observed, have to do with our duty to love and worship our Creator. The last six commandments have to do with our duty to man.

Our Lord summarized the two tables of the law when he answered the lawyer's question: 'Teacher, which is the great commandment in the law?' (*Matt.* 22:36). Jesus said to him, '"You shall love the LORD your God with all your heart, with all your soul, and with all your mind." This is the first and great commandment. And the second is like it: "You shall love your neighbor as yourself." On these two commandments hang all the Law and the Prophets' (*Matt.* 22:37–40).

The application of the Fifth Commandment extends much farther than to our natural parents. We have at least five kind of fathers: political fathers (the magistrate); grave, ancient men; spiritual fathers; domestic fathers (the house master); as well as natural fathers (fathers of the flesh).

In the Fifth Commandment are also included all superiors in age and gifts; and especially such as, by God's ordinance, are over us in the place of authority, whether in the family, the church, or the government.

DUTIES REQUIRED IN THE FIFTH COMMANDMENT

According to the *Larger Catechism*, 'The general scope of the Fifth Commandment is the performance of those duties which we mutually owe in our several relations, as inferiors, superiors, or equals' (Answer to Question 126).

The duty of honour to superiors:

('The honour which inferiors owe to their superiors is all due reverence in heart, word, and behaviour' – *Larger Catechism*, Answer to *Question* 127).

> You shall rise before the gray headed and honor the presence of an old man, and fear your God: I *am* the LORD (*Lev.* 19:32).

The duty to pray and give thanks for superiors:

> Therefore I exhort first of all that supplications, prayers, intercessions, *and* giving of thanks be made for all men, for kings and all who are in authority, that we may lead a quiet and peaceable life in all godliness and honesty (*1 Tim.* 2: 1–2).

The duty to imitate their virtues and graces:

> Remember those who rule over you, who have spoken the word of God to you, whose faith follow, considering the outcome of *their* conduct (*Heb.* 13:7).

The duty of willing obedience to the lawful commands of superiors:

> Children, obey your parents in the Lord, for this is right. 'Honor your father and mother,' which is the first commandment with promise . . . Bondservants, be obedient to those who are your masters according to the flesh, with

fear and trembling, in sincerity of heart, as to Christ; not with eyeservice, as men-pleasers, but as bondservants of Christ, doing the will of God from the heart, with goodwill doing service, as to the Lord, and not to men (*Eph.* 6:1–2, 5–7).

Listen to your father who begot you,
And do not despise your mother when she is old (*Prov.* 23:22).

'Listen now to my voice; I will give you counsel, and God will be with you: Stand before God for the people, so that you may bring the difficulties to God.' . . . So Moses heeded the voice of his father-in-law and did all that he had said (*Exod.* 18:19, 24).

Servants, *be* submissive to *your* masters with all fear, not only to the good and gentle, but also to the harsh. For this *is* commendable, if because of conscience toward God one endures grief, suffering wrongfully. For what credit *is it* if, when you are beaten for your faults, you take it patiently? But when you do good and suffer, if you take it patiently, this *is* commendable before God (*1 Pet.* 2:18–20).

The duty of due submission to correction:

Furthermore, we have had human fathers who corrected *us*, and we paid *them* respect. Shall we not much more readily be in subjection to the Father of spirits and live? (*Heb.* 12:9)

The duty of fidelity to superiors:

Exhort bondservants to be obedient to their own masters, to be well pleasing in all *things*, not answering back, not pilfering, but showing all good fidelity, that they may adorn the doctrine of God our Savior in all things (*Titus* 2:9–10).

The duty to defend superiors:

So David said to Abner, '*Are* you not a man? And who is like you in Israel? Why then have you not guarded your lord the king? For one of the people came in to destroy your lord the king. This thing that you have done *is* not good. *As* the LORD lives, you deserve to die, because you have not guarded your master, the LORD's anointed' (*1 Sam.* 26:15–16).

But the people answered, 'You shall not go out! For if we flee away, they will not care about us; nor if half of us die, will they care about us. But *you* are worth ten thousand of us now. For you are now more help to us in the city ' (*2 Sam.* 18:3).

And it was found written that Mordecai had told of Bigthana and Teresh, two of the king's eunuchs, the door-keepers who had sought to lay hands on King Ahasuerus (*Esther* 6:2).

The duty of bearing with the infirmities of superiors, covering them with love:

Servants, *be* submissive to *your* masters with all fear, not only to the good and gentle, but also to the harsh (*1 Pet.* 2:18).

But Shem and Japheth took a garment, laid *it* on both their shoulders, and went backward and covered the nakedness of their father. Their faces *were* turned away, and they did not see their father's nakedness (*Gen.* 9:23).

The duty of superiors to love, pray for, and bless inferiors:

Husbands, love your wives and do not be bitter toward them (*Col.* 3:19).

That they [older women] admonish the young women to love their husbands, to love their children (*Titus* 2:4).

Moreover, as for me, far be it from me that I should sin against the LORD in ceasing to pray for you; but I will teach you the good and the right way (*1 Sam.* 12:23).

So it was, when the days of feasting had run their course, that Job would send and sanctify them, and he would rise early in the morning and offer burnt offerings *according to* the number of them all. For Job said, 'It may be that my sons have sinned and cursed God in their hearts.' Thus Job did regularly (*Job* 1:5).

Then he stood and blessed all the assembly of Israel with a loud voice, saying: 'Blessed *be* the LORD, who has given rest to His people Israel, according to all that He promised. There has not failed one word of all His good promise, which He promised through His servant Moses' (*1 Kings* 8:55–58).

The duty of superiors to instruct inferiors:

And these words which I command you today shall be in your heart. You shall teach them diligently to your children, and shall talk of them when you sit in your house, when you walk by the way, when you lie down, and when you rise up (*Deut.* 6:6–7).

And you, fathers, do not provoke your children to wrath, but bring them up in the training and admonition of the Lord (*Eph.* 6:4).

The duty of superiors to reward inferiors when they do well.

Then the king said, 'What honor or dignity has been bestowed on Mordecai for this?' And the king's servants who attended him said, 'Nothing has been done for him' (*Esther* 6:3).

The duty of superiors to reprove and chasten inferiors:

The rod and rebuke give wisdom,
But a child left *to himself* brings shame to his mother (*Prov.* 29:15).

The duty of superiors to provide for inferiors:

But if anyone does not provide for his own, and especially for those of his household, he has denied the faith and is worse than an unbeliever (*1 Tim.* 5:8).

The duty of superiors to give a good example to inferiors:

The older women likewise, that they be reverent in behavior, not slanderers, not given to much wine, teachers of good things–that they admonish the young women to love their husbands, to love their children, to be discreet, chaste, homemakers, good, obedient to their own husbands, that the word of God may not be blasphemed (*Titus* 2:3–5).

SINS FORBIDDEN IN THE FIFTH COMMANDMENT:

The sin of neglecting the duties required of inferiors:

For God commanded, saying, 'Honor your father and your mother'; and, 'He who curses father or mother, let him be put to death.' But you say, 'Whoever says to his father or mother, "Whatever profit you might have received from me *is* a gift *to God*"—then he need not honor his father or mother.' Thus you have made the commandment of God of no effect by your tradition (*Matt.* 15:4–6).

The sin of rebellion against superiors:

After this it happened that Absalom provided himself with chariots and horses, and fifty men to run before him . . . Then Absalom sent spies throughout all the tribes of Israel, saying, 'As soon as you hear the sound of the trumpet, then you shall say, "Absalom reigns in Hebron!"' (*2 Sam.* 15:1, 10).

If a man has a stubborn and rebellious son who will not obey the voice of his father or the voice of his mother, and *who*, when they have chastened him, will not heed them, then his father and his mother shall take hold of him and bring him out to the elders of his city, to the gate of his city. And they shall say to the elders of his city, 'This son of ours is stubborn and rebellious; he will not obey our voice; he is a glutton and a drunkard.' Then all the men of his city shall stone him to death with stones; so you shall put away the evil from among you, and all Israel shall hear and fear (*Deut.* 21:18–21).

The sin of cursing or mocking superiors:

There is a generation *that* curses its father,
And does not bless its mother . . .
The eye *that* mocks his father,
And scorns obedience to *his* mother,
The ravens of the valley will pick it out,
And the young eagles will eat it (*Prov.* 30:11, 17).

He who mistreats *his* father *and* chases away *his* mother
Is a son who causes shame and brings reproach (*Prov.* 19:26).

The sin of neglecting the duties required of superiors:

Son of man, prophesy against the shepherds of Israel, prophesy and say to them, 'Thus says the LORD God to the shepherds: 'Woe to the shepherds of Israel who feed themselves! Should not the shepherds feed the flocks? You eat the fat and clothe yourselves with the wool: you slaughter the fatlings, *but* you do not feed the flock. The weak you have not strengthened, nor have you healed those who were sick, nor bound up the broken, nor brought back what was driven away, nor sought what was lost; but with force and cruelty you have ruled them' (*Ezek.* 34:2–4).

The sin of superiors who seek their own glory, ease, profit, and pleasure:

How can you believe, who receive honor from one another, and do not seek the honor that *comes* from the only God? (*John* 5:44).

He who speaks from himself seeks his own glory; but He who seeks the glory of the One who sent Him is true, and no unrighteousness is in Him (*John* 7:18).

His watchmen *are* blind,
They are all ignorant;
They *are* all dumb dogs,
They cannot bark;
Sleeping, lying down, loving to slumber.
Yes, *they are* greedy dogs
Which never have enough.
And they *are* shepherds
Who cannot understand;
They all look to their own way,
Every one for his own gain,
From his *own* territory (*Isa.* 56:10–11).

Neither shall he [the king] multiply wives for himself, lest his heart turn away; nor shall he greatly multiply silver and gold for himself (*Deut.* 17:17).

The sin of superiors who command unlawful actions:

Then a herald cried aloud: 'To you it is commanded, O peoples, nations, and languages, *that* at the time you hear the sound of the horn, flute, harp, lyre, *and* psaltery, in symphony with all kinds of music, you shall fall down and worship the gold image that King Nebuchadnezzar has set up; and whoever does not fall down and worship shall be cast immediately into the midst of a burning fiery furnace' (*Dan.* 3:4–6).

'But so that it spreads no further among the people, let us severely threaten them, that from now on they speak to no man in this name.' So they called them and commanded them not to speak at all nor teach in the name of Jesus (*Acts* 4:17–18).

The sin of superiors who dishonour themselves, or lessen their authority by unjust, indiscreet, rigorous, or remiss behaviour:

Then he drank of the wine and was drunk, and became uncovered in his tent (*Gen.* 9:21).

Then the king answered the people roughly, and rejected the advice which the elders had given him; and he spoke to them according to the advice of the young men, saying, 'My father made your yoke heavy, but I will add to your yoke; my father chastised you with whips, but I will chastise you with scourges!' So the king did not listen to the people; for the turn *of events* was from the LORD, that He might fulfill IIis word, which the LORD had spoken by Ahijah the Shilonite to Jeroboam the son of Nebat. Now when all Israel saw that the king did not listen to them, the people answered the king, saying: 'What share have we in David ? *We have* no inheritance in the son of Jesse. To your tents, O Israel! Now, see to your own house, O David!' So Israel departed to their tents (1 *Kings* 12:13–16).

Why do you kick at My sacrifice and My offering which I have commanded *in My* dwelling place, and honor your sons more than Me, to make yourselves fat with the best of all the offerings of Israel My people? Therefore the LORD God of Israel says: 'I said indeed *that* your house and the house of your father would walk before Me forever.' But now the LORD says: 'Far be it from Me; for those who honor Me I will honor, and those who despise Me shall be lightly esteemed' (1 *Sam.* 2:29–30).

The Sixth Commandment

You shall not murder
(Exod. 20:13).

Before we consider some of the specific duties required and sins forbidden by the Sixth Commandment, let me make some preliminary observations, at greater length than in the case of other commandments, so as to deal with some areas of current controversy.

The Sixth Commandment teaches a reverence for God's reign over human life. The basis for that authority is that He is the Creator of human life. He breathed into us the breath that gives us life; therefore, he has the right, the exclusive right, to take life. 'The LORD kills and makes alive; He brings down to the grave and brings up' (1 Sam. 2:6); 'You turn man to destruction, and say, "Return, O children of men"' (Psa. 90:3).

The Sixth Commandment is very broad because there are many ways in which murder is committed:

1. With the hands.
2. With the mind – malice is mental murder. 'Whoever hates his brother is a murderer, and you know that no murderer has eternal life abiding in him' (1 John 3:15).
3. With the tongue.

4. With the pen. David killed Uriah by writing to Joab
– 'And he wrote in the letter, saying, "Set Uriah in the
forefront of the hottest battle, and retreat from him,
that he may be struck down and die"' (*2 Sam.* 11:15).
5. By plotting the death of another.
6. By consenting to another's death. Paul consented to
Stephen's death, and later said, 'I persecuted this Way
to the death' (*Acts* 22:4).
7. By not hindering the death of another when it is
within our power to do so.
8. By not executing the law upon capital offenders.

The Sixth Commandment condemns suicide, regardless
of the high-sounding name it may be called, such as
voluntary death. How does this commandment require us
to deal with the sickly and the terminally ill, perhaps those
who are not blessed with a full quality of living? The
answer seems to be posed in a relatively new way today. It
is called *euthanasia*, dying easily, dying well. But it is an old
practice. Do not be fooled by those who act as though they
are on the edge of modernity. The ancient Spartans took
their unwanted babies and exposed them to the birds. The
ancient Romans took the elderly to the bridge over the
Tiber and threw them in. The most recent expression was
in the Third Reich. Hitler began by saying that he was
going to do away with only the very worst cases. But the
boundary kept moving back; the law of the avalanche set
in, and soon there was no distinguishable boundary at all.
Therefore, the Christian must oppose, at the very beginning, that wrong principle which says that human beings
have the right to decide the destiny of other human beings.
They do not! This is God's exclusive authority, and it may
not be taken by man! It is God alone who reigns over
human life.

The example of Samson (*Judges* 16:30) does not favour
suicide. This was a singular deed, carried out by the
extraordinary influence of the Holy Spirit, as appears from

Hebrews 11:34, which implies that Samson did this by faith, from the prayers which he offered to God for obtaining extraordinary strength for this act, and from his prayers being heard (*Judges* 16:28). God increased his strength and bestowed the desired success that he might thus be an illustrious type of Christ bringing great destruction upon the enemies of his people. Futhermore, the design was not simply private revenge, but the vindication of the glory of God, of religion, and of the people, since Samson was a public person and had been raised up by God from the people as an avenger.

A very important observation concerns abortion, which is murder in the womb. The emerging life in the womb begins at the union of the sperm and the ovum, which constitutes a human life. When a child is removed from the womb, the act is not like taking out an appendix or removing a tumour – it is extinguishing human life. Some may say that there would be great inconvenience in bearing this life. There might be embarrassment, financial inconvenience, disruption of schedules. But can any inconvenience justify the taking of human life? Others would say that there are sociological considerations; there are reasons of over-population, food supply and poverty. These are reasons that make it good for us to eliminate this child. But I want to ask, when did we begin to solve human problems by taking a human life? Refusing to yield to God's reign over life does not solve human problems.

Though the Lord visits and deals with every sin, yet he will, in a special manner, make inquisition for blood. 'When He avenges blood, He remembers them; He does not forget the cry of the humble' (*Psa.* 9:12). In Exodus 21:28 the Bible tells us that if a beast killed a man, it was to be stoned and its flesh was not to be eaten. If God would have a beast which killed a man stoned, though it had not the use of reason to restrain it, think how much more he is incensed with those who, against reason and conscience, murder unborn babies. There should be great lamentation in lands which are defiled with the blood of unborn babies. Oh, how common this sin is in our boastful age! Our sins are written in letters of blood. These are wholesale murders, and this should increase our lamentation. Abortion is a crying sin against the Sixth Commandment.

God said to Cain, who was the first murderer, 'The voice of your brother's blood cries out to Me from the ground.' Each drop of blood had a tongue, as it were, to cry aloud for vengeance. This sin of innocent blood lay heavily on David's conscience. Though he had sinned by adultery, what he cried out for most was the crime of shedding innocent blood: 'Deliver me from the guilt of bloodshed, O God' (*Psa.* 51:14).

Are the rights of war and punishment affected by this commandment? Since various cases can occur in which homicide can either be lawful or unlawful, the question arises, What is prohibited in the Sixth Commandment, and what is not?

First, negatively, judicial homicide is not prohibited, when carried out by the public magistrate against persons convicted of capital crimes. The magistrate is responsible to put the law into effect. He is armed with the sword for the purpose of avenging evil, 'For he is God's minister to you for good. But if you do evil, be afraid; for he does not bear the sword in vain; for he is God's minister, an avenger to *execute* wrath on him who practices evil' (*Rom.* 13:4). Governors are 'sent . . . for the punishment of evildoers and *for the* praise of those who do good' (*1 Pet.* 2:14). This pertains not only to heathen magistrates but to all magistrates as such, whether believers or not, though it has a special relevance to believers, who desire to see the law observed. This could not be done if they were not allowed to punish the guilty. For where there is no fear of punishment, crime is encouraged. Public security and peace could never be preserved if the sword could not be unsheathed against the guilty.

This public right is not opposed either by the Sixth Commandment, which respects private persons (not magistrates and ministers of God clothed with public authority), or by Christian charity, which can love the person and punish the crime. It would be a violation of the law of charity to leave the desperately wicked unpunished, since this would be injurious to the public good.

The right of war also belongs to the magistrate and can be lawfully exercised by him in a just and necessary war. However, unjust and hasty wars, undertaken without good and necessary cause, from ambition or avarice or in order to extend the boundaries of a country, are as detestable as mere highway robberies.

Several reasons can be given in defence of just wars:

First, war was lawful under the Old Testament and so remains lawful under the New, the reasons for it remaining in force. The very fact that Christ did not take away, but confirmed, the authority of the magistrate suggests that He approved of the right to carry on war, since it pertains to the magistrate to defend his people against unjust violence, which cannot always be done without war. Besides these matters fall under the moral and natural law, which was confirmed by Christ.

Secondly, the same right is repeatedly approved in the New Testament. John the Baptist, preparing the way of the Lord, sanctioned bylaws of military discipline (*Luke* 3:14). The soldiers asked him what they ought to do in order to escape the wrath to come and obtain eternal life. He did not order them to give up their military profession (which they would have had to do if it was wicked and unlawful *per se*), but told them that, remaining in it, they should be content with their wages and do violence to no man. If the military life were hateful to God under the New Testament, John would not have prescribed a rule for that life, but would have condemned it and exhorted the soldiers to change their occupation. Similarly, the faith of the centurion is commended by Christ (*Matt.* 8:10), and the piety of Cornelius is mentioned by Luke (*Acts* 10:1–2) and confirmed by the testimony of an angel (*Acts* 10:4). Also, Paul does not refuse to employ a military guard for his safety and protection (*Acts* 23:31).

Thirdly, the office of the magistrate may require him to wage war. He has been given the sword as the avenger of crimes (*Rom.* 13:4; *1 Pet.* 2:14). If small robberies, committed against a few, are rightly punished, how much more should great public robberies by those who endeavour to lay waste entire regions be punished? The magistrate is bound to undertake the defence of his people, to care for public peace and safety and to guard his country and its laws against those who strive to destroy them. This cannot be done without the right to wage just war.

When it is said: 'He shall judge between the nations, and rebuke many people; they shall beat their swords into plowshares and their spears into pruning hooks' (*Isa.* 2:4), the meaning is that the propagation of the kingdom of Christ is to be accomplished, not by carnal weapons, but by the preaching of the gospel and the power of the Holy Spirit alone. But it cannot be inferred that it is not lawful for the magistrate to carry on wars for just and necessary causes, since the gospel does not abolish governments or magistrates.

Although the weapons of the apostles with which they were to fight against Satan, the world and the flesh were said to be spiritual, not carnal (*2 Cor.* 10:4), because they were to make war against the world, not by external force, but by the preaching of the Word alone (*Matt.* 28:19–20); and although the weapons of believers in their spiritual warfare are prayers and tears, it does not follow that the right of the sword and of carnal weapons does not belong to the magistrate. As the calling of the apostles and of believers does not take away the office of the magistrate, so the spiritual weapons with which believers fight do not take away the carnal weapons the magistrate uses. The private duty of believers is one thing, the public duty of a magistrate another. Private believers ought to be prepared to shed their own blood rather than that of others because the right of the sword and of war is not granted to them. But it is different with the office of the magistrate. God has armed him for the avenging of wickedness and the defence of the state and the church. There is also granted to him the right of waging necessary wars.

Objections drawn from Matthew 5:39 and similar passages do not prove that every war is simply unlawful. What is said there is said to private persons. It is not said to the public authority ordained of God, a revenger to execute wrath upon him that does evil (*Rom.* 13:4). It is true that James teaches that the origin of wars is evil because it is always unjust on one side (*James* 4:1), but it does not follow that every war is evil on both sides. It is frequently lawful for the magistrate to repel and avenge offensive injury by force.

Taking life in self-defence is not forbidden when anyone, for the purpose of defending his own life against a violent and unjust aggressor, kills another. For this to be lawful self-protection, however, it is necessary that the aggressor unjustly assails us, that the defender has no other means of escape, that the defence is made during the very attack and not after it is over and that nothing is done by the defender either under the impulse of anger or with the desire of revenge, but with the sole intention of defending himself.

Although it is not lawful to return like for like and to avenge oneself, still to repel force by force and to defend oneself belongs to natural and perpetual right (especially where the aggression is simply violent and destitute of all public authority), even to the extent of slaying the aggressor, provided this is not intended for its own sake, but is the only way by which we can defend our lives and free ourselves from the unjust oppression.

However, it is wrong to extend such defence to the preservation or recovery of honour. Honour can be recovered, but life never can, and killing here would involve not lawful defence but unlawful revenge. But it does extend to the defence of life, whether our own or our neighbour's, especially when he is bound to us by a close tie, such as our parents, wife, children or friends. The person who does not repel an injury from another when he can is as much to blame as the one who commits it. Blameless protection is not prohibited in Romans 12:19, while private revenge is. Nor does the person who justly defends his own life do so as a private undertaking, but by the public authority of the law of nature.

The injunctions to love our enemies do not take away the necessary defence of life because the foundation of the love of neighbours is the love of ourselves. The passage in Matthew 26:52 in which our Lord orders Peter, 'Put your sword in its place, for all who take the sword will perish by the sword', does not take away just self-defence. Peter's action had the appearance more of rash anger than of defence, which would have been useless against so great a multitude. Again, he had not waited for the command of the Lord, who had no need of such a defender, but acted precipitately.

DUTIES REQUIRED IN THE SIXTH COMMANDMENT

The duty to preserve our own life:

So husbands ought to love their own wives as their own bodies; he who loves his wife loves himself. For no one ever hated his own flesh, but nourishes and cherishes it, just as the Lord *does* the church (*Eph.* 5:28–29).

The duty to preserve the life of others:

For so it was, while Jezebel massacred the prophets of the LORD, that Obadiah had taken one hundred prophets and hidden them, fifty to a cave, and had fed them with bread and water (*1 Kings* 18:4).

The duty to resist all thoughts and purposes and subdue all passions which tend to the unjust taking away of anyone's life:

'But know for certain that if you put me to death, you will surely bring innocent blood on yourselves, on this city, and on its inhabitants . . . ' So the princes and all the people said to the priests and prophets, 'This man does not deserve to die' (*Jer.* 26:15–16).

'This man was seized by the Jews and was about to be killed by them. Coming with the troops I rescued him, having learned that he was a Roman' (*Acts* 23:27).

'Be angry, and do not sin'; do not let the sun go down on your wrath, nor give place to the devil (*Eph.* 4:26–27).

My son, if sinners entice you,
Do not consent.
If they say, 'Come with us,
Let us lie in wait to *shed* blood;
Let us lurk secretly for the innocent without cause . . . '
My son, do not walk in the way with them,
Keep your foot from their path (*Prov.* 1:10–11, 15).

But Reuben heard *it*, and he delivered him out of their hands, and said, 'Let us not kill him' (*Gen.* 37:21).

The duty of just defence against violence:

Deliver the poor and needy;
Free *them* from the hand of the wicked (*Psa.* 82:4).

Deliver *those who* are drawn toward death,
And hold back *those* stumbling to the slaughter.
If you say, 'Surely we did not know this,'
Does not He who weighs the hearts consider *it*?
He who keeps your soul, does He *not* know it?
And will He *not* render to *each* man according to his deeds?
(*Prov.* 24:11–12).

But the people said to Saul, 'Shall Jonathan die, who has accomplished this great deliverance in Israel? Certainly not! As the LORD lives, not one hair of his head shall fall to the ground, for he has worked with God this day.' So the people rescued Jonathan, and he did not die (*1 Sam.* 14:45).

The duty to comfort the distressed and protect and defend the innocent:

Now we exhort you, brethren, warn those who are unruly, comfort the fainthearted, uphold the weak, be patient with all (*1 Thess.* 5:14).

If I have seen anyone perish for lack of clothing, or any poor *man* without covering; if his heart has not blessed me, and *if* he was *not* warmed with the fleece of my sheep . . . then let my arm fall from my shoulder, let my arm be torn from the socket (*Job* 31:19–20, 22).

For I was hungry and you gave Me food; I was thirsty and you gave Me drink; I was a stranger and you took Me in (*Matt.* 25:35).

Open your mouth for the speechless,
In the cause of all who *are* appointed to die.
Open your mouth, judge righteously,
And plead the cause of the poor and needy (*Prov.* 31:8–9).

SINS FORBIDDEN IN THE SIXTH COMMANDMENT

The sin of neglecting or withdrawing the lawful and necessary means of the preservation of life:

For I was hungry and you gave Me no food; I was thirsty and you gave Me no drink; I was a stranger and you did not take Me in, naked and you did not clothe Me, sick and in prison and you did not visit Me (*Matt.* 25:42–43).

If a brother or sister is naked and destitute of daily food, and one of you says to them, 'Depart in peace, be warmed and filled,' but you do not give them the things which are needed for the body, what *does* it profit? (*James* 2:15–16).

There is an evil which I have seen under the sun, and it *is* common among men: a man to whom God has given riches and wealth and honor, so that he lacks nothing for himself of all he desires; yet God does not give him power to eat of it, but a foreigner consumes it. This *is* vanity, and it *is* an evil affliction (*Eccles.* 6:1–2).

The sin of unjustified anger:

But I say to you that whoever is angry with his brother without a cause shall be in danger of the judgment. And whoever says to his brother, 'Raca!' shall be in danger of the council. But whoever says, 'You fool!' shall be in danger of hell fire (*Matt.* 5:22).

The sin of hatred:

Whoever hates his brother is a murderer, and you know that no murderer has eternal life abiding in him (*1 John* 3:15).

You shall not hate your brother in your heart. You shall surely rebuke your neighbour, and not bear sin because of him (*Lev.* 19:17).

The sin of envy:

A sound heart *is* life to the body,
But envy *is* rottenness to the bones (*Prov.* 14:30).

The sin of desiring revenge:

Beloved, do not avenge yourselves, but rather give place to wrath; for it is written, 'Vengeance is Mine, I will repay,' says the Lord (*Rom.* 12:19).

The sin of quarrelling:

But if you bite and devour one another, beware lest you be consumed by one another! (*Gal.* 5:15).

Who has woe?
Who has sorrow?
Who has contentions?
Who has complaints?
Who has wounds without cause?
Who has redness of eyes? (*Prov.* 23:29).

The sin of striking and wounding:

But if he strikes him with an iron implement, so that he dies,
he *is* a murderer; the murderer shall surely be put to death.
And if he strikes him with a stone in the hand, by which one
could die, and he does die, he *is* a murderer; the murderer
shall surely be put to death. Or *if* he strikes him with a
wooden hand weapon, by which one could die, and he does
die, he *is* a murderer; the murderer shall surely be put to
death (*Num.* 35: 16–18).

All of these sins have their roots in the Sixth Commandment, 'You shall not murder'.

A summary of this commandment may be helpful. 'You
shall not murder' is a very broad commandment. It
requires many duties and forbids many sins. Negatively, it
forbids every unlawful injury inflicted upon our own or our
neighbour's person. Our neighbour may be injured by
neglecting him or by not assisting him according to our
ability. Again, we may injure our neighbour by external
force or violence, but we may also break this commandment internally by anger, hatred or desire of revenge. Then
positively, this commandment requires the preservation of
our own and our neighbour's life and safety. This is done by
rendering assistance to others or by protecting them from
injuries, in a way of humanity, mercy or friendship.

The Seventh Commandment

You shall not commit adultery
(Exod. 20:14).

This commandment contains God's plan for preserving marriage. An excellent parallel passage for our meditation on the Seventh Commandment is this:

You cover the altar of the LORD with tears,
With weeping and crying;
So He does not regard the offering anymore,
Nor receive *it* with goodwill from your hands.
Yet you say, 'For what reason?'
Because the LORD has been witness
Between you and the wife of your youth,
With whom you have dealt treacherously;
Yet she is your companion
And your wife by covenant.
But did He not make *them* one,
Having a remnant of the Spirit?
And why one?
He seeks godly offspring.
Therefore take heed to your spirit,
And let none deal treacherously with the wife of his youth.

'For the LORD God of Israel says
That He hates divorce,
For it covers one's garment with violence,'
Says the LORD of hosts.
'Therefore take heed to your spirit,
That you do not deal treacherously.' (*Mal.* 2:13–16).

We must ever keep in mind that the commandments are gifts of God's love to us; they are not meant to inhibit our good or our joy, but to direct us to life abundant. In this commandment God is preserving marriage. The Seventh Commandment is a fence around marriage. God is committed to marriage.

DUTIES REQUIRED IN THE SEVENTH COMMANDMENT

The duty to be chaste in body, mind, and affections:

That each of you should know how to possess his own vessel in sanctification and honor (*1 Thess.* 4:4).

I have made a covenant with my eyes;
Why then should I look upon a young woman? (*Job* 31:1)

The duty to be chaste in words and behaviour:

Let your speech always *be* with grace, seasoned with salt, that you may know how you ought to answer each one (*Col.* 4:6).

When they observe your chaste conduct *accompanied* by fear (*1 Pet.* 3:2).

The duty to preserve chastity in ourselves and others:

Nevertheless, because of sexual immorality, let each man have his own wife, and let each woman have her own husband . . . And this I say for your own profit, not that I may put a leash on you, but for what is proper, and that you may serve the Lord without distraction. But if any man thinks he is behaving improperly toward his virgin, if she is past the flower of youth, and thus it must be, let him do what he wishes. He does not sin; let them marry (*1 Cor.* 7:2, 35–36).

The duty to keep chaste company:

To deliver you from the immoral woman,
From the seductress who flatters with her words,
Who forsakes the companion of her youth,
And forgets the covenant of her God.
For her house leads down to death,
And her paths to the dead;
None who go to her return,
Nor do they regain the paths of life—
So you may walk in the way of goodness,
And keep *to* the paths of righteousness (*Prov.* 2:16–20).

The duty to be modest in apparel:

In like manner also, that the women adorn themselves in modest apparel, with propriety and moderation, not with braided hair or gold or pearls or costly clothing (*1 Tim.* 2:9).

The duty of marriage by those that do not have the gift of continence:

But if they cannot exercise self-control, let them marry. For it is better to marry than to burn *with passion* (*1 Cor.* 7:9).

The duty of conjugal love:

And rejoice with the wife of your youth.
As a loving deer and a graceful doe,
Let her breasts satisfy you at all times;
And always be enraptured with her love.
For why should you, my son, be enraptured by an
    immoral woman,
And be embraced in the arms of a seductress?
(*Prov.* 5: 18–20).

The duty to resist temptation:

Remove your way far from her [the immoral woman],
And do not go near the door of her house (*Prov.* 5:8).

SINS FORBIDDEN IN THE SEVENTH COMMANDMENT

The sin of adultery and fornication:

Marriage *is* honorable among all, and the bed undefiled; but fornicators and adulterers God will judge (*Heb.* 13:4).

Now the works of the flesh are evident, which are: adultery, fornication, uncleanness, lewdness (*Gal.* 5:19).

The sin of rape and incest:

However, he would not heed her voice; and being stronger than she, he forced her and lay with her (*2 Sam.* 13:14).

It is actually reported *that there is* sexual immorality among you, and such sexual immorality as is not even named among the Gentiles—that a man has his father's wife! (*1 Cor.* 5:1).

The sin of sodomy and all unnatural lusts:

Therefore God also gave them up to uncleanness, in the lusts of their hearts, to dishonor their bodies among themselves . . . For this reason God gave them up to vile passions. For even their women exchanged the natural use for what is against nature. Likewise also the men, leaving the natural use of the woman, burned in their lust for one another, men with men committing what is shameful, and receiving in themselves the penalty of their error which was due (*Rom.* 1:24, 26–27).

If a man mates with an animal, he shall surely be put to death, and you shall kill the animal. If a woman approaches any animal and mates with it, you shall kill the woman and the animal. They shall surely be out to death. Their blood is upon them (*Lev.* 20:15–16).

The sin of unclean imaginations, thoughts, purposes, and affections:

But I say to you that whoever looks at a woman to lust for her has already committed adultery with her in his heart (*Matt.* 5:28).

For out of the heart proceed evil thoughts, murders, adulteries, fornications, thefts, false witness, blasphemies (*Matt.* 15:19).

Therefore put to death your members which are on the earth: fornication, uncleanness, passion, evil desire, and covetousness, which is idolatry (*Col.* 3:5).

The sin of corrupt or filthy communications:

But fornication and all uncleanness or covetousness, let it not even be named among you, as is fitting for saints; neither filthiness, nor foolish talking, nor coarse jesting, which are not fitting, but rather giving of thanks (*Eph.* 5:3–4).

That they may keep you from the immoral woman,
From the seductress *who* flatters with her words . . .
With her enticing speech she caused him to yield,
With her flattering lips she seduced him.
Immediately he went after her, as an ox goes to the
  slaughter,
Or as a fool to the correction of the stocks (*Prov.* 7:5,
21–22).

The sin of wanton looks:

Moreover the LORD says:
'Because the daughters of Zion are haughty,
And walk with outstretched necks
And wanton eyes,
Walking and mincing *as* they go,
Making a jingling with their feet . . . ' (*Isa.* 3:16).

Having eyes full of adultery and that cannot cease from sin, enticing unstable souls. *They have* a heart trained in covetous practices, and *are* accursed children (*2 Pet.* 2:14).

The sin of prohibiting lawful marriages:

Forbidding to marry, *and commanding* to abstain from foods which God created to be received with thanksgiving by those who believe and know the truth (*1 Tim.* 4:3).

The Seventh Commandment

The sin of disregarding unlawful marriages:

For John had said to Herod, 'It is not lawful for you to have your brother's wife' (*Mark* 6:18).

Judah has dealt treacherously,
And an abomination has been committed in Israel and in Jerusalem,
For Judah has profaned
The LORD's holy *institution* which He loves:
He has married the daughter of a foreign god.
May the LORD cut off from the tents of Jacob
The man who does this, being awake and aware,
Yet who brings an offering to the LORD of hosts! (*Mal.* 2: 11–12).

The sin of allowing, tolerating and keeping houses of prostitution or resorting to them:

And he banished the perverted persons from the land, and removed all the idols that his fathers had made (*1 Kings* 15:12).

Then he tore down the *ritual* booths of the perverted persons that *were* in the house of the LORD, where the women wove hangings for the wooden image (*2 Kings* 23:7).

There shall be no *ritual* harlot of the daughters of Israel, or a perverted one of the sons of Israel. You shall not bring the wages of a harlot or the price of a dog to the house of the LORD your God for any vowed offering, for both of these *are* an abomination to the LORD your God (*Deut.* 23:17,18)

Do not prostitute your daughter, to cause her to be a harlot, lest the land fall into harlotry, and the land become full of wickedness (*Lev.* 19:29).

How shall I pardon you for this ?
Your children have forsaken Me
And sworn by *those that are* not gods.

When I had fed them to the full,
Then they committed adultery
And assembled themselves by troops in the harlots' houses
(*Jer.* 5:7).

Now therefore, listen to me, *my* children;
Pay attention to the words of my mouth:
Do not let your heart turn aside to her [the harlot's] ways,
Do not stray into her paths;
For she has cast down many wounded,
And all who were slain by her were strong *men.*
Her house *is* the way to hell,
Descending to the chambers of death (*Prov.* 7:24–27).

The sin of having more than one spouse at the same time:

For this reason a man shall leave his father and mother and be joined to his wife, and the two shall become one flesh (*Matt.* 19:5).

The sin of unjust divorce:

'For the LORD God of Israel says
That He hates divorce,
For it covers one's garment with violence, '
Says the LORD of hosts.
'Therefore take heed to your spirit,
That you do not deal treacherously' (*Mal.* 2:16).

But I say to you that whoever divorces his wife for any reason except sexual immorality causes her to commit adultery; and whoever marries a woman who is divorced commits adultery (*Matt.* 5:32).

The sin of unchaste company:

So it was, as she spoke to Joseph day by day, that he did not heed her, to lie with her *or* to be with her (*Gen.* 39:10).

Remove your way far from her [the immoral woman],
And do not go near the door of her house (*Prov.* 5:8).

The sin of using words, pictures or actions which incite to uncleanness:

Neither filthiness, nor foolish talking, nor coarse jesting, which are not fitting, but rather giving of thanks (*Eph.* 5:4).

But she increased her harlotry;
She looked at men portrayed on the wall,
Images of Chaldeans portrayed in vermilion,
Girded with belts around their waists,
Flowing turbans on their heads,
All of them looking like captains,
In the manner of the Babylonians of Chaldea,
The land of their nativity.
As soon as her eyes saw them,
She lusted for them
And sent messengers to them in Chaldea (*Ezek.* 23:14–16).

And when Herodias' daughter herself came in and danced, and pleased Herod and those who sat with him, the king said to the girl, 'Ask me whatever you want, and I will give *it* to you' (*Mark* 6:22).

For we *have spent* enough of our past lifetime in doing the will of the Gentiles—when we walked in lewdness, lusts, drunkenness, revelries, drinking parties, and abominable idolatries (*1 Pet.* 4:3).

And *when* you *are* plundered,
What will you do?
Though you clothe yourself with crimson,
Though you adorn *yourself* with ornaments of gold,
Though you enlarge your eyes with paint,
In vain you will make yourself fair;
Your lovers will despise you;
They will seek your life (*Jer.* 4:30).

Furthermore you sent for men to come from afar, to whom a messenger *was* sent; and there they came. And you washed yourself for them, painted your eyes, and adorned yourself with ornaments (*Ezek.* 23:40).

Closing Thoughts on the Seventh Commandment

The ordinance of marriage should be observed. Let every man have his own wife, and let every woman have her own husband (*1 Cor.* 7:2).

Marriage is honourable and the bed undefiled (*Heb.* 13:4).

God instituted marriage in paradise (*Gen.* 2:22). He gave the man and the woman to each other in marriage.

Our Lord honoured marriage with his presence (*John* 2:1–11). The first miracle he wrought was at a marriage feast when he turned the water into wine.

Marriage is a type and resemblance of the mystical union between Christ and his church: '"For this reason a man shall leave his father and mother and be joined to his wife, and the two shall become one flesh." This is a great mystery, but I speak concerning Christ and the church' (*Eph.* 5:31–32).

'You shall not commit adultery.' This commandment needs to be proclaimed throughout the world today. We are living in a day when it is almost completely disregarded. Our promiscuous society has issued a challenge to Almighty God saying, 'I will do as I please, live as I please, practise what I please; therefore, stay out of my life with your Word and with your commandments.' Yet the holiness of God sets him against uncleanness.

Yes, the sins of fornication, homosexuality, and adultery against which our Lord spoke – the unlawful intercourse between unmarried men and women and between men and women who are married to another – have plunged our nations into a whirlpool of debauchery which is drowning precious souls by the million! The whole fabric of our society is so eaten up with this sin of lust that God may totally reject us as a society *unless there is repentance*. True repentance will show itself in the forsaking of this sin and crying to God for mercy through the Lord Jesus Christ.

The Eighth Commandment

You shall not steal
(Exod. 20:15).

J ust as we saw in the Seventh Commandment that the
holiness of God sets him against uncleanness, so we will
now see in the Eighth Commandment that the *justice* of
God sets him against theft and robbery. That which is
forbidden in this commandment is meddling with the
property of another. Theft is laying hands on that which
belongs to another – the invading of another's rights.

The Eighth Commandment is one of the most terse of
the commandments. In those four short words God has
encompassed so much that he wants to teach us about our
possessions and how to handle them. Does it not seem
embarrassingly obvious? 'You shall not steal.' Of course we
would not steal! That seems so clear and easy. But God has
a way of packing into the shortest, clearest little phrase so
much profound truth, expecting us to explain and expound
his commandments, drawing out of them the riches with
which he has loaded them.

DUTIES REQUIRED IN THE EIGHTH COMMANDMENT

The duty to be truthful, faithful and just in our contracts and commerce:

He who walks uprightly,
And works righteousness,
And speaks the truth in his heart . . .
In whose eyes a vile person is despised,
But he honors those who fear the LORD;
He *who* swears to his own hurt and does not change
(*Psa.* 15:2, 4).

Then the word of the LORD of hosts came to me, saying . . .
'Do not oppress the widow or the fatherless,
The alien or the poor.
Let none of you plan evil in his heart
Against his brother' (*Zech.* 7:4, 10).

'These *are* the things you shall do:
Speak each man the truth to his neighbor;
Give judgment in your gates for truth, justice, and peace;
Let none of you think evil in your heart against your neighbor;
And do not love a false oath.
For all these *are things* that I hate,'
Says the LORD (*Zech.* 8:16–17).

The duty to render to everyone his due:

Render therefore to all their due: taxes to whom taxes *are* due, customs to whom customs, fear to whom fear, honor to whom honor (*Rom.* 13:7).

The duty to make restitution of goods unlawfully obtained:

If a person sins and commits a trespass against the LORD by lying to his neighbor about what was delivered to him for safekeeping, or about a pledge, or about a robbery, or if he has extorted from his neighbor, or if he has found what was lost and lies concerning it, and swears falsely—in any one of these things that a man may do in which he sins: then it shall be, because he has sinned and is guilty, that he shall restore what he has stolen, or the thing which he has extorted, or what was delivered to him for safekeeping, or the lost thing which he found, or all that about which he has sworn falsely. He shall restore its full value, add one-fifth more to it, and give it to whomever it belongs, on the day of his trespass offering (*Lev.* 6:2–5; compare with *Luke* 19:8).

The duty to give and lend freely, according to our abilities and the necessities of others:

Give to everyone who asks of you. And from him who takes away your goods do not ask *them* back . . . Give, and it will be given to you: good measure, pressed down, shaken together, and running over will be put into your bosom. For with the same measure that you use, it will be measured back to you (*Luke* 6:30, 38).

But whoever has this world's goods, and sees his brother in need, and shuts up his heart from him, how does the love of God abide in him? (*1 John* 3:17).

Let him who stole steal no longer, but rather let him labor, working with *his* hands what is good, that he may have something to give him who has need (*Eph.* 4:28).

Therefore, as we have opportunity, let us do good to all, especially to those who are of the household of faith (*Gal.* 6:10).

The duty to be frugal:

So when they were filled, He said to His disciples, 'Gather up the fragments that remain, so that nothing is lost' (*John* 6:12).

There is desirable treasure,
And oil in the dwelling of the wise,
But a foolish man squanders it (*Prov.* 21:20).

The duty to further, by lawful means, the wealth of others as well as our own:

If one of your brethren becomes poor, and falls into poverty among you, then you shall help him, like a stranger or a sojourner, that he may live with you (*Lev.* 25:35).

If you meet your enemy's ox or his donkey going astray, you shall bring it back to him again (*Exod.* 23:4).

Let each of you look out not only for his own interests, but also for the interests of others (*Phil.* 2:4).

SINS FORBIDDEN IN THE EIGHTH COMMANDMENT

The sin of theft or robbery:

Let him who stole steal no longer, but rather let him labor, working with *his* hands what is good, that he may have something to give him who has need (*Eph.* 4:28).

Do not trust in oppression,
Nor vainly hope in robbery;
If riches increase,
Do not set *your* heart *on them* (*Psa.* 62:10).

The sin of receiving anything that is stolen:

Whoever is a partner with a thief hates his own life;
He swears to tell the truth, but reveals nothing (*Prov.* 29:24).

The sin of using false weights and measures:

Dishonest scales *are* an abomination to the LORD,
But a just weight is His delight (*Prov.* 11:1).

Diverse weights *and* diverse measures,
They *are* both alike, an abomination to the LORD (*Prov.* 20:10).

The sin of unfaithfulness in contracts:

'When will the New Moon be past, That we may sell grain?
And the Sabbath, That we may trade wheat?

Making the ephah small and the shekel large,
Falsifying the scales by deceit' (*Amos* 8:5).

The wicked borrows and does not repay,
But the righteous shows mercy and gives (*Psa.* 37:21).

The sin of extortion:

Woe to you, scribes and Pharisees, hypocrites! For you cleanse the outside of the cup and dish, but inside they are full of extortion and self-indulgence (*Matt.* 23:25).

'In you they take bribes to shed blood; you take usury and increase; you have made profit from your neighbors by extortion, and have forgotten Me,' says the Lord GOD (*Ezek.* 22:12).

The sin of usury:

He *who* does not put out his money at usury,
Nor does he take a bribe against the innocent.
He who does these *things* shall never be moved (*Psa.* 15:5).

The sin of bribery:

For the company of hypocrites *will be* barren,
And fire will consume the tents of bribery (*Job* 15:34).

The sin of taking or withholding from our neighbour what belongs to him:

For he has oppressed *and* forsaken the poor,
He has violently seized a house which he did not build (*Job* 20:19).

Indeed the wages of the laborers who mowed your fields, which you kept back by fraud, cry out; and the cries of the reapers have reached the ears of the Lord of Sabaoth (*James* 5:4).

Getting treasures by a lying tongue
Is the fleeting fantasy of those who seek death (*Prov.* 21:6).

The sin of idleness:

For we hear that there are some who walk among you in a disorderly manner, not working at all, but are busybodies (*2 Thess.* 2:11).

He who is slothful in his work
Is a brother to him who is a great destroyer (*Prov.* 18:9).

The Ninth Commandment

*You shall not bear false witness
against your neighbor*
(Exod. 20:16).

This commandment binds the tongue as to its
behaviour. Calvin remarks: 'Just as the previous
commandment ties the hands, so this one ties the tongue'
(*Brief Outline of the Christian Faith* (1537), newly trans-
lated by Stuart Olyott and published as *Truth for All Time*,
Edinburgh: Banner of Truth Trust, 1998, p. 20). The
Scripture calls slandering 'attacking with the tongue' (*Jer.*
18:18).

Augustine said, 'The tongue inflicts greater wounds than
the sword.' Thomas Watson adds, 'The wounds of the
tongue no physician can heal' (*The Ten Commandments*,
London: Banner of Truth Trust, 1965, p. 169). He goes on:
'As it is a sin against this commandment to raise a false
report of another, so it is to receive a false report before we
have examined it . . . He that raises a slander, carries the
devil in his tongue; and he that receives it, carries the devil
in his ear.' Watson shows that two things are particularly
forbidden in this commandment: slandering our neighbour

and false witness against our neighbour. Again, there are two kinds of false witness:

1. There is bearing false witness *for* another, where we give our witness for a person who is guilty.
2. There is bearing false witness *against* another, when we accuse a person falsely.

Watson encourages those who are falsely accused with this assertion: 'A good conscience is a wall of brass, that will be able to stand against a false witness. As no flattery can heal a bad conscience, so no slander can hurt a good one' (*The Ten Commandments*, p. 173), but, as he also points out, a man may wrong another as much by silence as by slander when he knows him to be wrongfully accused, yet does not speak in his behalf.

As before, the following duties required and sins forbidden are drawn from the *Larger Catechism*.

Duties Required in the Ninth Commandment

The duty of preserving and promoting truth and the good name of our neighbour:

These *are* the things you shall do:
Speak each man the truth to his neighbor;
Give judgment in your gates for truth, justice, and peace (*Zech*. 8:16).

Demetrius has a *good* testimony from all, and from the truth itself. And we also bear witness, and you know that our testimony is true (*3 John* 12).

The duty to stand for the truth and to do so from the heart:
Open your mouth for the speechless,
In the cause of all *who are* appointed to die.
Open your mouth, judge righteously,
And plead the cause of the poor and needy (*Prov*. 31:8–9).

He who walks uprightly,
And works righteousness,
And speaks the truth in his heart (*Psa*. 15:2).

The duty to speak the truth and only the truth in matters of judgment and justice:

You shall do no injustice in judgment. You shall not be partial to the poor, nor honor the person of the mighty. In righteousness you shall judge your neighbor (*Lev.* 19:15).

A faithful witness does not lie,
But a false witness will utter lies . . .
A true witness delivers souls,
But a deceitful *witness* speaks lies (*Prov.* 14:5, 25).

The duty to speak the truth at all times:

Therefore, when I was planning this, did I do it lightly? Or the things I plan, do I plan according to the flesh, that with me there should be Yes, Yes, and No, No? But *as* God *is* faithful, our word to you was not Yes and No (*2 Cor.* 1:17–18).

Therefore, putting away lying, 'Let each one of you speak truth with his neighbor,' for we are members of one another (*Eph.* 4:25).

The duty of rejoicing in the gifts and graces of others:

First, I thank my God through Jesus Christ for you all, that your faith is spoken of throughout the whole world (*Rom.* 1:8).

Greatly desiring to see you, being mindful of your tears, that I may be filled with joy, when I call to remembrance the genuine faith that is in you, which dwelt first in your grandmother Lois and your mother Eunice, and I am persuaded is in you also (*2 Tim.* 1:4–5).

I rejoiced greatly that I have found *some* of your children walking in truth, as we received commandment from the Father (*2 John* 4).

For I rejoiced greatly when brethren came and testified of the truth *that is* in you, just as you walk in the truth. I have no greater joy than to hear that my children walk in truth (*3 John* 3–4).

The duty to receive a good report of others:

[Love] does not rejoice in iniquity, but rejoices in the truth; bears all things, believes all things, hopes all things, endures all things (1 Cor. 13:6–7).

The duty to discourage all talebearers, flatterers and slanderers:

The north wind brings forth rain,
And a backbiting tongue an angry countenance (Prov. 25:23).

He who hates, disguises it with his lips,
And lays up deceit within himself;
When he speaks kindly, do not believe him,
For there are seven abominations in his heart (Prov. 26: 24–25).

Whoever secretly slanders his neighbor,
Him I will destroy; The one who has a haughty look and a proud heart,
Him I will not endure (Psa. 101:5).

The duty to keep lawful promises:

He who swears to his own hurt and does not change (Psa. 15:4).

The duty to study and practise everything true, noble, lovely and of good report:

Finally, brethren, whatever things are true, whatever things are noble, whatever things are just, whatever things are pure, whatever things are lovely, whatever things are of good report, if there is any virtue, and if there is anything praiseworthy—meditate on these things (Phil. 4:8).

SINS FORBIDDEN IN THE NINTH COMMANDMENT

The sin of partiality in judging, especially in courts of law:

You shall do no injustice in judgment. You shall not be

partial to the poor, nor honor the person of the mighty. In righteousness you shall judge your neighbour (*Lev.* 19:15).

The sin of giving false evidence:

A false witness will not go unpunished,
And *he who* speaks lies will not escape (*Prov.* 19:5).

These six *things* the LORD hates,
Yes, seven *are* an abomination to Him . . .
A false witness *who* speaks lies,
And one who sows discord among brethren (*Prov.* 6: 16, 19).

The sin of passing an unjust sentence, calling evil good and good evil:

He who justifies the wicked, and he who condemns the just,
Both of them alike *are* an abomination to the LORD (*Prov.* 17:15).

Who justify the wicked for a bribe,
And take away justice from the righteous man! (*Isa.* 5:23).

The sin of lying:

In transgressing and lying against the LORD,
And departing from our God,
Speaking oppression and revolt,
Conceiving and uttering from the heart words of falsehood (*Isa.* 59:13).

The proud have forged a lie against me,
But I will keep Your precepts with *my* whole heart (*Psa.* 119:69).

You shall not steal, nor deal falsely, nor lie to one another (*Lev.* 19:11).

Do not lie to one another, since you have put off the old man with his deeds (*Col.* 3:9).

The sin of concealing the truth:

If a person sins in hearing the utterance of an oath, and *is* a witness, whether he has seen or known *of the matter*—if he does not tell *it*, he bears guilt (*Lev.* 5:1).

You shall not consent to him or listen to him, nor shall your eye pity him, nor shall you spare him or conceal him (*Deut.* 13:8).

And he kept back part of the proceeds . . . and brought a certain part and laid it at the apostles' feet. But Peter said, 'Ananias, why has Satan filled your heart to lie to the Holy Spirit and keep back *part* of the price of the land for yourself? (*Acts* 5:2–3).

The sin of speaking the truth unseasonably:

A fool vents all his feelings,
But a wise *man* holds them back (*Prov.* 29:11).

The sin of perverting the truth to a wrong meaning:

All day they twist my words;
All their thoughts *are* against me for evil (*Psa.* 56:5).

Jesus answered and said to them, 'Destroy this temple, and in three days I will raise it up' (*John* 2:19). But at last two false witnesses came forward and said, 'This fellow said, "I am able to destroy the temple of God and to build it in three days."' (*Matt.* 26:60–61).

The sin of slandering and backbiting:

You sit *and* speak against your brother;
You slander your own mother's son (*Psa.* 50:20).

He *who* does not backbite with his tongue,
Nor does evil to his neighbor,
Nor does he take up a reproach against his friend (*Psa.* 15:3).

The sin of talebearing:

You shall not go about *as* a talebearer among your people (*Lev.* 19:16).

The sin of misconstruing intentions, words, and actions:

It is reported among the nations, and Geshem says, *that* you and the Jews plan to rebel; therefore, according to these rumors, you are rebuilding the wall, that you may be their king. And you have also appointed prophets to proclaim concerning you at Jerusalem, saying, '*There is* a king in Judah!' . . . Then I sent to him, saying, 'No such things as you say are being done, but you invent them in your own heart' (*Neh.* 6:6–8).

And *why* not say, 'Let us do evil that good may come'?—as we are slanderously reported and as some affirm that we say. Their condemnation is just (*Rom.* 3:8).

Now Hannah spoke in her heart; only her lips moved, but her voice was not heard. Therefore Eli thought she was drunk . . . But Hannah answered and said, 'No, my lord, I *am* a woman of sorrowful spirit. I have drunk neither wine nor intoxicating drink, but have poured out my soul before the LORD' (*1 Sam.* 1:13, 15).

And the princes of the people of Ammon said to Hanun their lord, 'Do you think that David really honors your father because he has sent comforters to you? Has David not *rather* sent his servants to you to search the city, to spy it out, and to overthrow it?' (*2 Sam.* 10:3).

The sin of flattery:

They speak idly everyone with his neighbor;
With flattering lips *and* a double heart they speak.
May the LORD cut off all flattering lips,
And the tongue that speaks proud things (*Psa.* 12:2–3).

. . . flattering people to gain advantage (*Jude* 16).

The sin of thinking too highly or too meanly of ourselves or others:

Also He spoke this parable to some who trusted in themselves that they were righteous, and despised others . . . The

Pharisee stood and prayed thus with himself, 'God, I thank You that I am not like other men—extortioners, unjust, adulterers, or even as this tax collector' (*Luke* 18:9, 11).

Be of the same mind toward one another. Do not set your mind on high things, but associate with the humble. Do not be wise in your own opinion (*Rom.* 12:16).

Then Moses said to the LORD, 'O my Lord, I *am* not eloquent, neither before nor since You have spoken to Your servant; but I *am* slow of speech and slow of tongue.' So the LORD said to him, 'Who has made man's mouth? Or who makes the mute, the deaf, the seeing, or the blind? *Have* not I, the LORD? Now therefore, go, and I will be with your mouth and teach you what you shall say.' But he said, 'O my Lord, please send by the hand of whomever *else* You may send.' So the anger of the LORD was kindled against Moses . . . (*Exod.* 4:10–14).

The sin of exaggerating minor faults:

And why do you look at the speck in your brother's eye, but do not consider the plank in your own eye? Or how can you say to your brother, 'Let me remove the speck from your eye', and look, a plank is in your own eye? Hypocrite! First remove the plank from your own eye, and then you will see clearly to remove the speck from your brother's eye (*Matt.* 7:3–5).

The sin of hiding or excusing sins, when called to a free confession:

He who covers his sins will not prosper,
But whoever confesses and forsakes *them* will have mercy (*Prov.* 28:13).

Then the man said, 'The woman whom You gave *to be* with me, she gave me of the tree, and I ate.' And the LORD God said to the woman, 'What *is* this you have done?' The woman said, 'The serpent deceived me, and I ate' (*Gen.* 3:12–13).

Then the LORD said to Cain, 'Where *is* Abel your brother?'

He said, 'I do not know. *Am* I my brother's keeper?' (*Gen.* 4:9).

The sin of raising false rumours:

You shall not circulate a false report. Do not put your hand with the wicked to be an unrighteous witness (*Exod.* 23:1).

The sin of groundless suspicion:

[Love] . . . thinks no evil . . . (*1 Cor.* 13:5).

. . . disputes and arguments over words, from which come . . . evil suspicions . . . (*1 Tim.* 6:4).

The sin of envying anyone's deserved credit:

Then Moses said to him, 'Are you zealous for my sake? Oh, that all the LORD's people were prophets *and* that the LORD would put His Spirit upon them!' (*Num.* 11:29).

But when the chief priests and scribes saw the wonderful things that He did, and the children crying out in the temple and saying, 'Hosanna to the Son of David!' they were indignant and said to Him, 'Do you hear what these are saying?' (*Matt.* 21:15–16).

The sin of scornful contempt and mocking:

But in my adversity they rejoiced
And gathered together;
Attackers gathered against me,
And I did not know it;
They tore *at me* and did not cease . . .
They also opened their mouth wide against me,
And said, 'Aha, aha!
Our eyes have seen it' (*Psa.* 35:15, 21).

And they stripped Him and put a scarlet robe on Him. When they had twisted a crown of thorns, they put *it* on His head, and a reed in His right hand. And they bowed the knee before Him and mocked Him, saying, 'Hail, King of the Jews!' (*Matt.* 27:28–29).

The Tenth Commandment

You shall not covet your neighbor's house;
you shall not covet your neighbor's wife,
nor his male servant, nor his female servant,
nor his ox, nor his donkey, nor anything
that is your neighbor's
(Exod. 20:17).

Before we consider some of the duties required and sins forbidden by the Tenth Commandment, it will be helpful to make some general comments and observations about its distinctiveness.

There are several synonyms for *covet*. The most accurate synonym is desire, or desire ardently; others include lust, long for, yearn, pine and crave inordinately. To covet is to wish for something with eagerness.

Coveting is not always evil. The Bible teaches us that we are earnestly to covet the best gifts (*1 Cor.* 12:31, AV). We are to covet the Lord Jesus Christ and a holy life.

The Importance of the Tenth Commandment

The Bible says that covetousness ('the love of money') is the root of all evil (*1 Tim.* 6:10). This is enough to make the

Tenth Commandment extremely important. It is important because:

1. It goes to the heart, the inner man.

2. It is spiritual: 'For we know that the law is spiritual, but I am carnal, sold under sin ' (*Rom.* 7:14).

3. It teaches us how the other commandments are meant to be interpreted; that is, the others are not just dealing with externals – they deal with thoughts as well as acts. The legalistic Jews missed this point. That is what our Lord is teaching them in the Sermon on the Mount (*Matt.* 5:20–48).

4. It has convicting power. It was the commandment that God used in Paul's conversion: 'What shall we say then? *Is* the law sin? Certainly not! On the contrary, I would not have known sin except through the law. For I would not have known covetousness unless the law had said, "*You shall not covet.*" But sin, taking opportunity by the commandment, produced in me all *manner of evil* desire. For apart from the law sin was dead. I was alive once without the law, but when the commandment came, sin revived and I died' (*Rom.* 7:7–9).

The great apostle was a blameless man (not sinless). He was scrupulous in his efforts to keep the commandments of God, so he thought he had kept them from his youth up. He had never worshipped any God but Jehovah; he had never done homage to any idols; he had never taken God's name in vain; he had never worked on the Sabbath; he honoured his father and his mother; he was never guilty of murder, adultery or theft. But when he began to reflect on the Tenth Commandment, which forbade him to covet, he discovered he had broken it flagrantly – he was 'sold under sin'. In many respects the Tenth Commandment is the greatest and most significant of all the commandments. Without the Tenth Commandment we would not realize that *all* the commandments are spiritual and go to the heart, the thoughts, the inner man.

All sins come from within: 'For from within, out of the heart of men, proceed evil thoughts, adulteries, fornications, murders, thefts, covetousness, wickedness, deceit, lewdness, an evil eye, blasphemy, pride, foolishness. All these evil things come from within and defile a man' (*Mark* 7:21–23).

This commandment condemns seeking things by dishonest means, that is, without labour, as in theft, gambling or lotteries.

Duties Required in the Tenth Commandment

The duty to be content with our own condition:

Let *your* conduct be without covetousness; *be* content with such things as you have. For He Himself has said, 'I will never leave you nor forsake you' (*Heb.* 13:5).

Now godliness with contentment is great gain (*1 Tim.* 6:6).

The duty to have a charitable attitude towards our neighbour, so that we desire his good:

Rejoice with those who rejoice, and weep with those who weep (*Rom.* 12:15).

Peace *be* within your walls,
Prosperity within your palaces.
For the sake of my brethren and companions,
I will now say, 'Peace be within you. '
Because of the house of the LORD our God
I will seek your good (*Psa.* 122: 7–9).

Now the purpose of the commandment is love from a pure heart, *from* a good conscience, and *from* sincere faith (*1 Tim.* 1:5).

For Mordecai the Jew *was* second to King Ahasuerus, and was great among the Jews and well received by the multitude of his brethren, seeking the good of his people and speaking peace to all his countrymen (*Esther* 10:3).

Love suffers long *and* is kind; love does not envy; love does not parade itself, is not puffed up; does not behave rudely, does not seek its own, is not provoked, thinks no evil; does not rejoice in iniquity, but rejoices in the truth; bears all things, believes all things, hopes all things, endures all things (*1 Cor.* 13:4–7).

SINS FORBIDDEN IN THE TENTH COMMANDMENT

The sin of discontent with what is ours:

So Ahab went into his house sullen and displeased because of the word which Naboth the Jezreelite had spoken to him; for he had said, 'I will not give you the inheritance of my fathers.' And he lay down on his bed, and turned away his face, and would eat no food (*1 Kings* 21:4).

'Yet all this avails me nothing, so long as I see Mordecai the Jew sitting at the king's gate' (*Esther* 5:13).

Nor complain, as some of them also complained, and were destroyed by the destroyer (*1 Cor.* 10:10).

The sin of envying and grieving at the good of our neighbour:

Let us not become conceited, provoking one another, envying one another (*Gal.* 5:26).

But if you have bitter envy and self-seeking in your hearts, do not boast and lie against the truth. This wisdom does not descend from above, but *is* earthly, sensual, demonic. For where envy and self-seeking *exist*, confusion and every evil thing *are* there (*James* 3:14–16).

He has dispersed abroad,
He has given to the poor;
His righteousness endures forever;
His horn will be exalted with honor.
The wicked will see it and be grieved;

He will gnash his teeth and melt away;
The desire of the wicked shall perish (*Psa.* 112:9–10).

When Sanballat the Horonite and Tobiah the Ammonite official heard *of it*, they were deeply disturbed that a man had come to seek the well-being of the children of Israel (*Neh.* 2:10).

The sin of inordinate desire for anything that is our neighbour's:

What shall we say then? *Is* the law sin? Certainly not! On the contrary, I would not have known sin except through the law. For I would not have known covetousness unless the law had said, *'You shall not covet.'* But sin, taking opportunity by the commandment, produced in me all *manner of evil* desire. For apart from the law sin *was* dead (*Rom.* 7:7–8).

For the commandments, *'You shall not commit adultery,'* *'You shall not murder,'* *'You shall not steal,'* *'You shall not bear false witness,'* *'You shall not covet,'* and if *there is* any other commandment, are *all* summed up in this saying, namely, *'You shall love your neighbor as yourself'* (*Rom.* 13:9).

Therefore put to death your members which are on the earth: fornication, uncleanness, passion, evil desire, and covetousness, which is idolatry (*Col.* 3:5).

Let Thomas Watson summarize what covetousness really is:

Covetousness is the root of discontent. Why do any repine at their condition, but because they think they do not have enough? The Greek word for covetousness signifies an immoderate desire of getting. Covetousness is a dry dropsy, and because the thirst is not satisfied, therefore the heart frets through discontent and impatience.

Covetousness is the root of theft. Achan's covetous humour made him steal that wedge of gold which served to cleave asunder his soul from God (*Josh.* 7:21).

Covetousness is the root of treason. It made Judas betray Christ. 'What will ye give me and I will deliver him unto you?' (*Matt.* 26:16). Absalom's covetousness made him attempt to pluck the crown from his father's head. He that is a Demas will soon prove a Judas. 'Men shall be covetous' (2 *Tim.* 3:2), and it follows in the next verse, 'traitors'. Where covetousness is in the premises, treason will be in the conclusion.

Covetousness is the root of murder. Why did Ahab stone Naboth to death but to possess his vineyard? (*1 Kings* 21:13). Covetousness has made many swim to the crown in blood. And can the heart be pure when the 'hands are full of blood'? (*Isa.* 1:15).

Covetousness is the root of perjury. 'Men shall be covetous', and it follows, 'truce breakers' (2 *Tim.* 3:2–3). For love of money [men] will take a false oath and break a just oath. He that lives a Midas will die a perjurer . . .

Covetousness is the root of bribery and injustice. It makes the courts of judicature 'great places of robbery', as Augustine speaks. At Athens causes were bought and sold for money.

It is the cause of uncleanness. The Scripture mentions 'the hire of a whore' (*Deut.* 23:18). For money both conscience and chastity are set to sale.

Covetousness is the root of idolatry: 'Covetousness which is idolatry' (*Col.* 3:5). The covetous person bows down to the image of gold. His money is his god, for he puts his trust in it. Money is his creator. When he has abundance of wealth, then he thinks he is made. It is his redeemer. If he be in any strait or trouble, he flies to his money and that must redeem him. It is his comforter. When he is sad he counts over his money and with this golden harp he drives away the evil spirit. When you see a covetous man, you may say, 'There goes an idolater.'

(*The Beatitudes,* London: Banner of Truth Trust, 1971, pp. 179–180).

One theologian called the Tenth Commandment 'God's Call to Contentment'. Contentment is the absolute antidote for covetousness.

Conclusion

Moreover the law entered that the offense might abound. But where sin abounded, grace abounded much more'
(Rom. 5:20).

We have considered the duties required by the Ten Commandments, and surely all will agree that no person has performed or can perform these duties. There is no power in the commandments to perform the duties required. We have considered the sins forbidden in the Ten Commandments, and must admit that we are guilty! We find no power in the commandments to enable us not to sin. Therefore, again we must say that we are guilty law-breakers and have no hope of being saved by perfectly obeying the Ten Commandments. Likewise, the law of ceremonies was never intended to save anyone. The ceremonies were pictures to set forth the way of salvation; but ceremonies were not themselves the way but a map, a model of the road but not the road itself. When the Ten Commandments were announced by God, he knew that everyone to whom he gave them had already broken them and could not claim justification by keeping them. He never intended the Ten Commandments to be a way of salvation. In fact, He had revealed his covenant of grace and the way of faith hundreds of years earlier to his servant Abraham. The Ten Commandments were not meant to negate, replace, or change the ancient assertion: *'Abraham believed God, and it was accounted to him for righteousness'* (*Rom.* 4:3). 'The just shall live by faith' (*Rom.* 1:17).

God sent the commandments into the world and addressed them to every creature so that an offence might be seen to be an offence. The commandments increase the sinfulness of sin by removing all excuses and ignorance of our duty. The commandments do not make us sinful, but they do display our sinfulness. In the presence of this perfect standard we see our imperfections, our shortcomings, yes, our sinfulness.

Thus, the commandments become like a mirror by which we can see the spots of dirt on our face, but we do not wash our face with the mirror. Just so, the commandments do not make us clean; they show us that we need cleansing and prompt us to seek cleansing. Our Saviour is the only one who can change us. He alone can say, 'You are already clean because of the word which I have spoken to you' (*John* 15:3). He alone has the water that cleanses. He said to the poor sinful woman at Jacob's well, 'Whoever drinks of the water that I shall give him will never thirst' (*John* 4:14). Reader, if you come short of Christ, you miss the intent and design of the Ten Commandments. Romans 5:20 makes it very clear that God gave the law so that the offence might be seen and felt to be an offence, and might abound.

The following statements can be taken as axioms, as things self-evident:

There can be no grace where there is no guilt.

There can be no mercy where there is no sin.

There can be just benevolence, but there cannot be mercy unless there is criminality.

Conclusion

If you are not a sinner, God cannot have mercy upon you, because where misery is not felt, mercy will not be regarded.

If you have never sinned, God cannot display pardoning mercy toward you for there is nothing to pardon.

It is double-talk to speak of forgiving a man who has done no wrong or of bestowing undeserved favour upon a person who deserves reward.

It would be an insult to innocence to offer it mercy. None will seek mercy until he first pleads guilty. Then, only the free, rich, sovereign grace of God can save him.

One of the principal purposes of the Ten Commandments is to show sinners that they have sinned and have need of forgiveness, pardon, grace, and mercy. We can preach forgiveness, mercy, and grace until we are hoarse, but those who think that they have never broken the law and are not guilty will never embrace our message of grace and forgiveness found only in Jesus Christ and Him crucified.

Let me ask, who can lay his own character down side by side with the two tablets of divine precepts without at once being convinced that he has fallen far short of that holy standard of righteousness? Our comeliness utterly fades away when the commandments shine their spiritual light on us. On the other hand, a proper use of the law will make a person always hold tenaciously to salvation by grace alone. The Ten Commandments show every creature that all have sinned and need a Saviour.

Study each commandment separately as to our duty to our Creator and to our fellow creatures and as to our sins against the Judge of all the earth. As you study each precept separately, you will find that in these ten short precepts you have all the moral virtues, the full compass of your accountability to your Maker and your neighbour. The essence of all just decrees and statutes is found in the Ten Commandments.

If the whole human race had kept the Ten Commandments, not violating one, the law would not stand in so splendid a position of honour as it does today when the man Christ Jesus has rendered satisfaction to it. God incarnate has in his life, and yet more in his death, revealed the supremacy of the law; He has shown that not even sovereignty can set aside justice. Who shall say a word against the law to which the Lawgiver himself submits? God the Father demanded the perfection of the law from His own dear Son.

In a sermon on Galatians 3:24–25 entitled 'The Stern Pedagogue', C. H. Spurgeon made the following statement:

And remember, last of all, that the law which is so sharp and terrible to men when it only deals with them for their good, will, if you and I die without being brought to Christ, be much more terrible to us in eternity, when it deals with us in justice for our punishment. Then it will not be enshrined in the body of Moses, but, terrible to tell, it will be incarnate in the person of the Son of God sitting upon the throne. He will be at once the Lawgiver, the Judge, and the Saviour; and you that have despised him as the Saviour will have to appear before him as your Judge. No such judge as he, his justice will be clear and undiluted now that his mercy has been scorned. Oil is soft, but set it on fire, and see how it burns! Love is sweet, but curdle it to jealousy, and see how sour it is! If you turn the Lamb of Zion into the Lion of the tribe of Judah, beware, for he will tear you in pieces, and there shall be none to deliver. Rejected love will change its hand. The pierced hand was outstretched with invitations of mercy, but if these be rejected – Oh, sirs, I am telling you solemn truth, and hear it, I pray you, ere I send you away – if, from that hand that was pierced, you will not take the perfect salvation which he is prepared to give to all who confess their guilt, you will have to receive from that self-same hand the blows of that iron rod which shall break you in pieces as a potter's vessel. Fly now and kiss the Son, lest he be angry, and ye perish from the way when his wrath is kindled but a little. Blessed are all they that put their trust in him! Amen.

Before I conclude, let me issue a solemn call and invitation to all the poor lawbreakers who read these words. Be sure of this, you will not get to heaven by keeping the commandments; you are a guilty lawbreaker and need pardon, forgiveness, and mercy. Any serious consideration of the Ten Commandments will make every honest person cry out, 'Oh, the load of guilt that is on my soul! My head and my heart are full of sin. Oh, my sins! Every commandment takes hold upon me; how great then is the sum of my guilt!'

The commandments should cause every lawbreaker to cry out, 'Come, Lord Jesus. Come quickly to my rescue. Save me, Lord, or I will perish.'

Our Lord's invitations are as wide as the needs of man. Let me quote just one such invitation:

Ho! Everyone who thirsts,
Come to the waters;
And you who have no money,
Come, buy and eat.
Yes, come, buy wine and milk
Without money and without price . . .
Incline your ear, and come to Me.
Hear, and your soul shall live;
And I will make an everlasting covenant with you—
The sure mercies of David (*Isa.* 55:1, 3).

Only Christ can save you from the hand of justice. He alone will be your protection from the arm of the law. Oh, reader, if you have any pity for your poor, perishing soul, close with the present offers of mercy. Do not shut the doors of mercy against yourself, but rather repent and be converted.

OTHER BANNER OF TRUTH TITLES: